GENDER AND SOCIETY

GENDER AND SOCIETY

*Essays Based on Herbert Spencer
Lectures Given in the University
of Oxford*

Edited by

COLIN BLAKEMORE
*Waynflete Professor of Physiology and
Fellow of Magdalen College.*

SUSAN IVERSEN
*Professor of Experimental Psychology and Fellow of
Magdalen College.*

OXFORD
UNIVERSITY PRESS

OXFORD

UNIVERSITY PRESS

Great Clarendon Street, Oxford OX2 6DP

Oxford University Press is a department of the University of Oxford.
It furthers the University's objective of excellence in research, scholarship,
and education by publishing worldwide in

Oxford New York

Athens Auckland Bangkok Bogotá Buenos Aires Calcutta
Cape Town Chennai Dar es Salaam Delhi Florence Hong Kong Istanbul
Karachi Kuala Lumpur Madrid Melbourne Mexico City Mumbai
Nairobi Paris São Paulo Singapore Taipei Tokyo Toronto Warsaw

and associated companies in Berlin Ibadan

Oxford is a registered trade mark of Oxford University Press
in the UK and certain other countries

Published in the United States
by Oxford University Press Inc., New York

British Library Cataloguing in Publication Data

Data available

Library of Congress Cataloging in Publication Data

Gender and society: the Herbert Spencer lectures / edited by Colin Blakemore,
Susan Iversen.

Includes bibliographical references and index.

1. Sex role. 2. Sex differences. 3. Women—Social conditions. I. Blakemore, Colin.
II. Iversen, Susan D., 1940–

HQ1075 .G4619 2000 305.3—dc21 99-057194

ISBN 0-19-829792-0

1 3 5 7 9 10 8 6 4 2

Typeset by Best-set Typesetter Ltd., Hong Kong
Printed in Great Britain
on acid-free paper by
T. J. International Ltd
Padstow, Cornwall

CONTENTS

LIST OF FIGURES

LIST OF TABLES

LIST OF CONTRIBUTORS

PETER N. GOODFELLOW has a career history that spans sex and drugs. As an academic, he studied sex determination in humans and as an industrialist, with SmithKline Beecham, he is searching for new pharmaceutical agents to treat disease. When he retires, Dr Goodfellow will concentrate on 'Rock and Roll'.

GERMAINE GREER is Professor of English and Comparative Studies at the University of Warwick. Her most recent book, *The Whole Woman*, was first published in England in March 1999. Her study of John Wilmot Earl of Rochester for the Writers and Their Work series will appear in February. An edition of the Works of Anne Finch Countess of Winchilsea, which she is preparing with her co-editor Hannah Smith will be published in 2000.

SARAH BLAFFER HRDY, Emeritus Professor of Anthropology, University of California-Davis. She has just published *Mother Nature: A history of natural selection, mothers, and infants*. Hrdy has been elected to the U.S. National Academy of Sciences and is a Fellow of the Animal Behavior Society, the California Academy of Sciences, and the American Academy of Arts and Sciences. She is currently writing a book on why people have children.

LUCIA JACOBS is an Assistant Professor in the Department of Pscyhology, University of California at Berkeley, where she is also a faculty member of the Institute for Cognitive Science and the Wills Neuroscience Institute.

MICHÉLE LE DOEUFF, Directrice de recherches in philosophy at the CNRS (Pairs) and former Professor Ordinaire in women's studies at Geneva University. Her books published in English are *The Philosophical Imaginary* and *Hipparchia's Choice. An Essay Concerning Women, Philosophy, etc.*

SUSAN COTTS WATKINS, Professor of Sociology and Associate of the Population Studies Centre at the University of Pennsylvania. She has written on fertility declines in Europe, in the United States, and Africa.

Sex and Molecular Biology

PETER N. GOODFELLOW

When I was fourteen, I was in love with Rowena and Rowena was in love with Stirling. This was not a *ménage à trois* since Stirling was a horse and he did not love me. Rowena attempted to resolve our mutual frustrations by introducing me to her friends. On one occasion, Rowena displayed me before Gabrielle. There was no immediate spark that suggested the possibility of future furtive explorations in the back row of the local cinema, but Gabrielle and I did agree to a 'date'. We met for a daring cup of coffee and attempted conversation.

'What do you do?' asked Gabrielle.
The obvious answer was that I was a schoolboy; clearly something more sophisticated was needed.
'I'm a biologist.'
The presumption of my youth was immediately exposed by Gabrielle's next remark
'My father is a biologist, he discovered the structure of DNA.'
'What?'
'You know—the helix, the double helix.'
My blank expression was repaid by disdain and the relationship was

I have been very fortunate in the last 15 years to have been able to exploit—I hope it has been mutual—a very talented group of scientists. I thank them for tolerating my idiosyncrasies. The work that led to the identification of *SRY* and equating it with *TDF* was part of a collaboration between my group and that of Dr Robin Lovell-Badge. My work has been generously supported by the Imperial Cancer Research Fund, the Medical Research Council, and the Wellcome Trust.

finished before a single attempted grope. I sometimes replay that scene and substitute a more sophisticated reply:

'Amazing work! It convinced me of the importance of model-building in structural analyses.'

Perhaps I could have been Francis Crick's son-in-law.

Today, a fourteen year old, with aspirations to be a biologist, would not fail the coffee bar DNA test. The structure of DNA (deoxyribonucleic acid) is arguably the most important scientific discovery ever made in Britain and is a defining totem of the twentieth century. DNA represents power. Your DNA makes you a human instead of a horse. Your DNA makes predictions about your future. If you inherit the mutation for Huntington's disease you will suffer and die from a very unpleasant disease, always assuming another catastrophe does not intervene. It is, however, easy to overstate the case. Growth, behaviour and well-being depend on an interplay between the environment and the individual. Each of us is a product of both DNA and environment. For any specific character, the relevant contribution of genes may be small or large and correspondingly difficult or easy to discern.

Until the work of Watson and Crick, genetics was largely the preserve of mathematicians interested in formulating the rules of inheritance. The beautiful structure of DNA provided the explanation of how information was stored by living things and how this information was transferred from generation to generation. Living things are made of units called cells. In the same way that bricks make a building and buildings can be made of many different types of bricks, we are made of cells. Cells are made of proteins. Unlike bricks in a building, each cell carries all the instructions for making both itself and all the other cells in the body. These instructions are carried in DNA and are encoded. DNA is made of two strands which coil around each other to form a double helix. Each strand is made of bases joined together like links in a chain. There are four types of bases: A, T, C, and G. The bases are paired on the two strands such that A is always paired with T and C with G. This means that each strand can act as the template for the other strand—hence, copying information is an essential part of replication. The order of the bases encodes information in groups of three: each triplet specifies an amino acid and amino acids are used to make proteins. A gene is that piece of DNA that codes for a single protein. The DNA in each cell is organized into chromosomes and is found in the nucleus. The DNA is transcribed into a messenger molecule called mRNA (a single-stranded molecule chemically related to DNA and also made of bases). The information in mRNA is translated and used to make proteins. In humans there are about 100,000 genes which code for 100,000 proteins. Putting those proteins together makes cells and makes us.

Humans are wonderfully diverse with many variations in size, shape, and colour. Some of this variety is due to differences in single genes but much is due to the interactions of many genes: the blue eye–brown eye variation is due to a single gene, however, multiple gene interactions cause other eye colour variations. Genetic diseases occur when DNA sustains damage which alters the sequence of the bases resulting either in the production of a protein with the wrong amino acids or the failure to produce any protein at all.

In classical genetics, physical characters are used as 'genetic markers' and their inheritance is followed in families. Unfortunately, most human variation is not under single gene control but is controlled by many genes and the inheritance pattern is too complex to discern. This makes it impossible to use physical characters, such as hair colour, skin colour, height, and weight, as genetic markers to follow inheritance in families. In 1980, the world of human genetics changed when classical genetics was combined with molecular biology and it was realized that variation at the level of DNA could be exploited as a virtually unlimited source of genetic markers. It has been estimated that more than 1 in every 1,000 base pairs of the human genome differs on average between any two individuals; as the human genome is composed of 3,000,000,000 base pairs there are a potential

3,000,000 genetic markers available for studying human genetics. This plethora of markers is driving human genetics and has facilitated the investigation of human health and disease.

Sex, the biological separation into male and female, is controlled by DNA and is determined by DNA. Gender, the arbitrary social division between masculine and feminine, is a social construct that involves interaction between an individual and society. The work of my laboratory has been focused on identifying the genetic basis of how sex is determined in mammals. Understanding gender will require a wide variety of skills and the contribution of the geneticist will not be the largest.

Sex, rabbits, and chromosomes

In a series of brilliant surgical experiments, many of which were performed during the German occupation of Paris in the Second World War, Alfred Jost demonstrated that testes produce factors that induce male development [1]. From experiments conducted on rabbit embryos *in utero*, Jost found that a castrated male embryo develops both a female reproductive tract and external female genitalia. A castrated female embryo also develops female features. These results implied that ovaries are not needed for female differentiation but that the formation of the testes is essential for male sex determination. As the testes and ovaries both derive from the same embryonic structure known as the gonadal ridge, Jost's experiments reduced the problem of sex determination to understanding how the gonads are chosen. The masculinizing effect of the testis is largely due to two hormones: *testosterone* and *anti-Müllerian hormone* (AMH is also commonly known as Müllerian inhibiting substance, MIS) [2].

These observations can be summarized as the first rule of mammalian sex determination: *the specialization of the developing gonad determines the subsequent sexual differentiation of the embryo.* The choice between forming a testis or an ovary is the process of sex determination; the process during and after gonad formation is called sex differentiation.

Sex determination in humans and other mammals is chromosomally based: normal females have two X chromosomes and males have an X and a Y chromosome. Individuals with a single X chromosome are female and individuals with multiple X chromosomes and a Y chromosome are male [3–5]. This provides the second rule of mammalian sex determination: *the Y chromosome carries genetic information required for testis formation.* For simplicity, the testis-determining activity of the Y chromosome was referred to as if it were a single gene and named *TDF* (testis determining factor) in man and *Tdy* (testis determining Y-gene) in mouse. In theory, Y chromosome control of sex determination could be due to the Y-location of all the genes required for testis development or the Y-location of a regulatory gene that interacts with genes elsewhere in the genome. As discussed below, we now know that *TDF* is a single gene and that this gene acts as the rate limiting step in the male sex determination pathway. Nevertheless, it is worth stressing that contributions from many genes are needed to make a testis.

Sex, sex-reversal, and SRY

It is a common theme in genetics that unusual phenotypes can be used to identify genes. Among both humans and mice, there are rare individuals who violate the rule that links the presence of the Y chromosome with testis determination: these exceptions include both males without a Y chromosome and females with a Y chromosome. XX males and XY females are described as 'sex-reversed'. Individuals with hormonal defects may present with ambiguous genitalia or inappropriate genitalia for their genotypes; these patients have defects in sexual differentiation and are not 'sex-reversed'.

Peter N. Goodfellow

Two competing hypotheses could explain the existence of XX males: either theses males have inherited cryptic sequences of bases derived from the Y chromosome or they have mutations in genes that respond to the presence of the Y-located testis-determining gene. Both hypotheses are correct: about 85 per cent of XX males have Y chromosome sequences in their genomes and the rest have mutations elsewhere in the sex-determination pathway. The XX males with Y chromosome material have suffered an unusual exchange of sequence between the X and Y chromosomes [6] (Fig. 1.1).

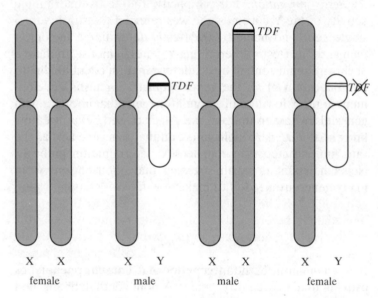

X   X   X   Y   X   X   X   Y

female   male   male   female

FIG. 1.1. Sex chromosomes of sex-reversed individuals. On the left are shown sex chromosomes of normal individuals (XX female and XY male) with the position of *TDF* indicated towards the end of the short arm of the Y chromosome. Exchange of genetic material normally occurs between the tips of the short arms of the X and Y chromosomes during male meiosis. Occasionally additional Y chromosome sequence including *TDF* is aberrantly transferred to the X. An XX individual with such an X chromosome is male, sex-reversed due to the presence of *TDF* (XX male). Inactivation of *TDF* by mutation results in male to female sex reversal (XY female).

Logic demands that they must have also inherited *TDF*. By screening many different XX males for the amount of Y sequence present, 4 XX males were identified, who had only 35,000 out of the 30,000,000 base pairs that make up the Y chromosome [7]. Within the 35,000 base pairs there was only one small gene, which was given the anodyne name *Sex-determining Region Y chromosome gene* or *SRY* (following mouse genetic nomenclature rules, the same gene in the mouse is known as *Sry*). The region of *SRY* that codes for protein is less than 1,000 base pairs [8, 9].

SRY, *sex-reversal, and mice*

Several circumstantial lines of evidence support the contention that *SRY* is the sex-determining gene *TDF*. *SRY* homologues are present on the Y chromosome in all eutherian and metatherian mammals tested [10]. The putative protein produced by *SRY* has the ability to bind to DNA [11]. This is consistent with a role for *SRY* as a regulator that controls the expression of other genes. In the mouse, the expression of *Sry*, during formation of the embryo, is limited to the gonadal ridge, the structure that gives rise to the gonads immediately before and during the beginning of testis formation [12]. These results paint a compelling picture, but the avid reader of detective stories will recognize the dangers of relying on circumstantial evidence. The direct evidence proving that *SRY* is the sex-determining gene is genetic. It is a strong prediction that mutations in the Y-located sex determining gene should result in XY females. In fulfillment of this prediction, about 15 per cent of XY females have dysfunctional *SRY* genes and the majority of these individuals have mutations that are not shared with their fathers [13]. These results prove that *SRY* is required for testis formation but do not prove that it is the only gene on the Y chromosome needed for sex determination.

Gene function can be tested directly by adding or

removing genes from the genomes of mice to produce 'transgenic' mice. A very simple experiment proved that *Sry* is the only sex determining gene on the Y chromosome. A female mouse embryo, with two X chromosomes, was injected with purified DNA which included *Sry* but no other genes. The result, although predicted, was remarkable: the XX mouse developed as a male mouse [14]. The transgenic mouse had testes and external male genitalia; in all respects he was male including his willingness and success in copulation with female mice. His only unusual feature was the small size of his testes. Histological examination showed that he did not produce sperm. There are two causes of this failure of spermatogenesis: first, for reasons that are not clearly understood, having two X chromosomes is incompatible with successful male meiosis and, second, the Y chromosome contains at least three genes that are needed for sperm morphogenesis. The lack of fertility and the spermatogenic defect were not unexpected as human XX males have exactly the same phenotype. *SRY* is the only gene on the Y chromosome needed for male sex determination.

SRY, SOX9, *and more genes*

What is the difference between men and women? At the level of DNA the answer is simple—*SRY*. This does not mean, however, that only *SRY* is needed to make a male. *SRY* acts in concert with many other genes; however, these genes are shared by males and females. It is the differential expression of these shared genes that produces either ovaries or testes. The identification of other genes involved in the process of sex determination and the elucidation of how they interact is a priority of current research. Genes that have been implicated include:

SOX9. The *SOX* genes are related to *SRY* and code for DNA binding proteins, there may be as many as a hundred

SOX genes in the human genome. Mutations in one of the *SOX* genes, *SOX9*, cause the rare disease, campomelic dysplasia [15, 16]. Patients afflicted with campomelic dysplasia suffer from generalized bone and cartilage disorders and usually die soon after birth from rupture of the trachea. About two-thirds of the affected XY patients are sex-reversed. It is not clear how the diverse phenotypic consequences of mutations in *SOX9* are related. The significance of the relationship between *SRY* and *SOX9* is also enigmatic.

SF1. Several genes in the steroid production pathways are regulated by *SF1* (*steroidogenesis factor 1*). Unexpectedly, *SF1* may also regulate AMH production [17] and mice that lack *SF1* fail to produce either gonads or adrenals [18].

WT1. Mutations in the Wilm's tumour suppressor gene result in the formation of embryonic tumours in kidneys. Two pieces of evidence link *WT1* with sex determination. First, mice with no functional *WT1* die during prenatal development and lack both kidneys and gonads [19]. Second, patients with Denys–Drash syndrome, which is caused by specific mutations in *WT1* [20], have renal insufficiency, Wilm's tumour, and can suffer problems in both sex determination and differentiation.

DSS. The presence of two active copies of part of the short arm of the X chromosome can result in XY sex reversal [21]. Recent work has suggested that the *dosage sensitive sex-determining gene* (*DSS*), is the same as the X-linked *adrenal hypoplasia gene* (*AHC*) and *DAX1*, a candidate gene for both syndromes has been identified [22]. *DAX1* encodes an orphan member of the nuclear hormone receptor superfamily. Deletion and mutation at *DAX1* causes X-linked adrenal hypoplasia but does not affect sex determination in males. One active copy in males and females produces a normal phenotype. Two copies of the region of the genome that includes *DAX1* in XY individuals results in ovarian development. It has been suggested that the normal function of *DSS* is as part of an ovarian determination pathway and that it may act as an inhibitor of *SRY*.

9

A working model of how some of these relationships might look is presented in Fig. 1.2. Although several of the players have been identified, the script is obscure. Who talks to whom, where and when remains to be learned before we have a complete understanding of how sex determination works.

SRY *and sexism in science*

Most research is carried out by and controlled by men. The possibility of sexism creeping unnoticed into scientific concepts is high. In one description of sex determination, the basic body plan of a mammal is female and this passive, default form is changed into the male form by the active male principle. In another description, the default form is male and *DSS* activates the female pattern and inhibits testis formation. In this case, *SRY* is a repressor of a repressor. It will be possible to distinguish between these two views of the world

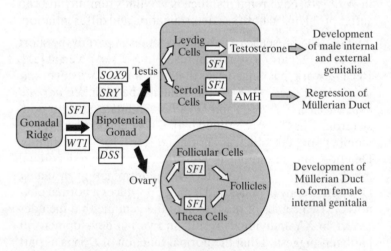

FIG. 1.2. Possible roles of genes so far known to be involved in the pathway of sex determination and sex differentiation.

and I look forward to knowing the answer but as a statement of belief, I think it is just as interesting to know how to make a woman as how to make a man—and, ever since my first non-love Rowena and my non-tryst with Gabrielle, I have had a profound interest in both sexes.

REFERENCES

1. JOST, A. *et al.* 'Studies on sex differentiation in mammals'. *Recent Progress in Hormone Research*, 1973, **29**: 1–41.

2. JOST, A. 'Studies on sex differentiation in mammals.' *Recent Progress in Hormone Research*, 1953, **8**: 379–418.

3. FORD, C. E. *et al.* 'A sex chromosome anomaly in a case of gonadal sex dysgenesis (Turner's syndrome)'. *Lancet*, 1959, **i**: 711–13.

4. JACOBS, P. A. and J. A. STRONG. 'A case of human intersexuality having a possible XXY sex-determining mechanism'. *Nature (London)*, 1959, **183**: 302–3.

5. WELSHONS, W. J. and L. B. RUSSELL, 'The Y-chromosome as bearer of male determining factors in the mouse'. *Proceedings of the National Academy of Science (USA)*, 1959, **45**: 560–6.

6. PETIT, C. *et al.* 'An abnormal terminal exchange accounts for most but not all cases of human XX maleness'. *Cell*, 1987, **49**: 595–602.

7. PALMER, M. S. *et al.* 'Genetic evidence that ZFY is not the testis-determining factor'. *Nature*, 1989, **342**: 937–9.

8. SINCLAIR, A. H. *et al.* 'A gene from the human sex-determining region encodes a protein with homology to a conserved DNA-binding motif'. *Nature*, 1990, **346**: 240–4.

9. GUBBAY, J. *et al.* 'A gene mapping to the sex-determining region of the mouse Y chromosome is a member of a novel family of embryonically expressed genes'. *Nature*, 1990, **346**: 245–50.

10. FOSTER, J. W. *et al.* 'Evolution of sex determination and the Y chromosome: SRY-related sequences in marsupials'. *Nature*, 1992, **359**: 531–3.

11. HARLEY, V. R. *et al.* 'DNA binding activity of recombinant SRY from normal males and XY females'. *Science*, 1992, **255**: 453–6.

12. KOOPMAN, P. *et al.* 'Expression of candidate sex-determining gene during mouse testis differentiation'. *Nature*, 1990, **348**: 450–2.

13. BERTA, P. *et al.* 'Genetic evidence equation SRY and the testis-determining factor'. *Nature*, 1990, **348**: 448–50.

14. KOOPMAN, P. *et al.* 'Male development of chromosomally female mice transgenic for Sry'. *Nature*, 1991, **351**: 117–21.

15. FOSTER, J. W. *et al.* 'Campomelic dysplasia and autosomal sex reversal caused by mutations in an SRY-related gene'. *Nature*, 1994, **372**: 525–30.

16. WAGNER, T. *et al.* 'Autosomal sex reversal and campomelic dysplasia are caused by mutations in and around the SRY-related gene SOX9'. *Cell*, 1994, **79**: 1111–20.

17. SHEN, W. H. *et al.* 'Nuclear receptor steroidogenic factor 1 regulates the Müllerian inhibiting substance gene: A link to the sex determination cascade'. *Cell*, 1994, **77**: 651–61.

18. LUO, X., Y. IKEDA, and K. L. PARKER. 'A cell-specific nuclear receptor is essential for adrenal and gonadal development and sexual differentiation'. *Cell*, 1994, **77**: 481–90.

19. KREIDBERG, J. A. *et al.* 'WT-1 is required for early kidney development.' *Cell*, 1993, **74**: 679–91.

20. PELLETIER, J. *et al.* 'Germline mutations in the Wilms' tumor suppressor gene are associated with abnormal urogenital development in Denys–Drash syndrome'. *Cell*, 1991, **67**: 437–47.

21. SCHERER, G. *et al.* 'Duplication of an Xp segment that includes the ZFY locus causes sex inversion in man.' *Human Genetics*, 1989, **81**: 291–4.

22. ZANARIA, E. *et al.* 'An unusual member of the nuclear hormone receptor superfamily responsible for X-linked adrenal hypoplasia congenita'. *Nature*, 1994, **372**: 635–41.

2

Gender and Population

SUSAN COTTS WATKINS

For the lecture honouring Herbert Spencer, I was invited to talk about gender and science. I am going to discuss fertility declines, a notable example of population change in the last century and a half. There will be three themes: first, the way that understandings of gender have influenced explanations of fertility declines offered by analysts of population change; second, how understandings of gender have influenced the efforts of international population activists to promote fertility declines in developing countries; and third, how local understandings of gender in western Kenya are currently influencing fertility change there. However, I start with a brief description of past demographic changes, first with the pervasive fertility declines in Europe in the latter half of the nineteenth century, and then the widespread onset of fertility declines in developing countries in the period after the second World War. These fertility declines were accomplished by profound alterations in reproductive behaviour. They constitute, I think, a far-reaching social change, one that I see as equivalent in their interest to other social changes such as the Protestant Reformation or the Industrial Revolution. Although I will focus on explanations, fertility declines have had important consequences, both for individuals and for societies.

What might account for fertility declines? Not surprisingly, many explanations have been offered. These explanations, I will suggest, often draw on our understandings of the social as well as the biological differences between men and women. Some of these explanations are frankly gendered: thus, in the nineteenth and early twentieth century some students of population proposed that the declines of fertility they observed were due to the preferences of women—often portrayed as over-educated or selfish—for engaging in activities other than childbearing and child-rearing. Other explanations, such as the more recent attempts to link the processes of economic development with consequences in bedroom behaviour, appear on the surface to be gender-neutral, but they nonetheless expose our conceptions of the differences between men and women.

I will then turn to international efforts to induce fertility decline in developing countries. The declines in fertility in Europe and the countries of European settlement were largely accomplished without modern techniques of family planning, and in the face of neutrality or opposition by societal institutions such as governments, churches, and the medical profession. This is not the case in developing countries, which to a considerable extent have become part of a global community linked by ties of trade, migration, communication, and media, as well as by the institutional ties of colonial and then international bureaucracies. Stimulated in the 1950s and 1960s by fears of a 'population crisis' brewing in developing countries, international institutions and western aid agencies expended a great deal of effort to persuade the governments of developing countries to adopt policies to reduce population growth by lowering fertility, and expended a great deal of money to support family planning programmes in these countries. These programmes were clearly influenced by conceptions of gender: women were targeted, men almost completely ignored.

Lastly, I shift focus, turning from the global visions of analysts in universities and activists in national and international agencies to examine the understandings of gender by men and women who are currently participating in the first stages of fertility transition in Kenya, where I worked a few years ago. In a remote area in western Kenya, on the shores of Lake Victoria, men and women are engaged in community-level debates about the advantages and disadvantages of smaller or larger numbers of children, and about the pros and cons of modern contraception. In these patrilineal, polygynous, and patriarchal areas where cattle are exchanged for women, most men and many women are sure that reproductive decisions should be made by women. Since the early 1980s, however, Kenya has had an aggressive national family planning programme, largely funded by outside donors, and targeted at women. These programmes have thus permitted those local women who wish to use family planning without the permission or the knowledge of their husband to do so, and thus to subvert the traditional gender balance of power.

Describing fertility transitions

Fertility declines in Europe were well described by the Princeton European Fertility Project (Coale and Watkins 1986). Ansley Coale and his colleagues calculated demographic measures for approximately 600 provinces (e.g. the counties of England, the *départements* of France, the cantons of Switzerland) from approximately 1870 to 1960.

In 1870, it appears that most women bore children from marriage to menopause (Henry 1961; Knodel 1983; Bongaarts and Menken 1983; Wilson 1984; Coale 1986). Some individuals may have deliberately attempted to stop bearing children before the end of the physiological period of childbearing, but there were not enough successful 'stoppers' to affect aggregate measures. The major exception is France, where fertility declines had begun at the national level around the time of the French Revolution and had been preceded by fertility declines in some areas (south-west France) and among some groups in other countries as well as France (e.g. aristocracies, Jews, some urban populations) even before that. (The United States is another exception: fertility decline there appears to have begun in the first quarter of the nineteenth century). The absence of deliberate attempts to stop childbearing does not mean, however, that marital fertility was uniform. Variations across provinces were substantial, but they were due to practices, such as extended breastfeeding, which do not appear to be associated with desires to reduce the number of children born in a marriage.[1]

After 1870, this situation changes substantially. By 1930, marital fertility had fallen by approximately 50 per cent across the provinces of Europe. Fertility transitions began in north-west Europe between 1870 and 1900, followed by the countries of central Europe and the Mediterranean, and then by Ireland and Albania.[2] Even more interesting is the evidence that, with few exceptions, once marital fertility had declined by 10 per cent, it continued to decline until very low levels of fertility were reached (Watkins 1986). It is as if a Pandora's box had been opened: once opened, once fertility control had caught on, it was apparently impossible to return to the earlier situation of continued childbearing from marriage to menopause. These changes occurred in countries that differed substantially from one another on a variety of dimensions. Historians make their living by studying national (or sometimes even smaller) populations, under the assumption that differences in levels of development, in political

---

[1] Outside of France, fertility was, to use a term introduced by Louis Henry, 'natural' (i.e. couples did not adjust their reproductive behaviour to the number of children they had already borne). For most parts of Europe, we do not have the sort of data that would permit us to determine for certain whether fertility was 'natural'. For England, however, we have the outstanding study of Tony Wrigley and Roger Schofield of the Cambridge Group. Using data from parish registers of baptisms, they were able to show that there was little evidence of deliberate control of fertility from 1600 to 1799 (Wrigley and Schofield 1983). Extrapolating from England, the participants in the Princeton European Fertility project concluded that there was little deliberate fertility control elsewhere.

[2] If we could examine areas smaller than provinces or if we had data on individuals, we would probably see that there was considerable fertility control among some in the decade or so before 1870 (Guinnane, Okun, and Trussell 1994).

systems, in culture, and in national history matter a lot. Such differences, however, appear to have played a relatively minor role in fertility transitions, typically affecting the timing of the onset by a few decades more or less.

The fertility declines were not only pervasive but rapid. If our measure is the onset of an irreversible fertility decline, marked by a 10 per cent decline in marital fertility, most of the action at the provincial and national levels occurred between 1870 and 1900; if our measure is a decline of 50 per cent, it occurred within sixty years; if our measure is a fall in fertility from about five or six children per couple to about two, the decline took about a century. This might not seem rapid; nonetheless, when we consider that there was apparently little change in marital fertility in the preceding centuries (see, for example, the comprehensive study of England's demographic history by Wrigley and Schofield 1983), the picture is of an abrupt and rapid change in bedroom behaviour. The changes also had profound conseqences for individuals and for societies. With fewer children, for example, men and women spend fewer years with young children in the home, more with opportunities for activities that might conflict with childrearing; women face lower risks of mortality and morbidity associated with childbearing; the age structure of the population changes, with a higher proportion of elderly.

The pattern of change is similar in some respects when we turn to the developing countries (Watkins 1987). There again we have little evidence of deliberate control of fertility on the national level before a certain period, in this case the 1950s (although it is likely that, as in Europe, some groups had begun this transformation earlier). There was a period of widespread public alarm in the west about rates of population growth in the developing world—a 'population crisis', a 'population bomb'. Mortality had fallen substantially but fertility had not, leading to growth rates that implied rapid doubling of these populations. Beginning in the 1940s, and reaching a crescendo in the 1960s and early 1970s (Wilmoth and Ball 1992), in academic journals as well as in the popular press, this was seen to herald a crisis, with implications variously for the political security of the globe, for famine, and, perhaps most prominently, for prospects that poor developing countries could develop economically.

As the west worried, however, fertility was beginning to decline. Between the early 1960s (1960–5) and the late 1980s (1985–90), the total fertility rate of the developing world declined by an estimated 36 per cent—from 6.0 to 3.8 births per woman (Bongaarts and Watkins 1996; United Nations, 1995). Declines have been most rapid in Asia and Latin America (–42 and –43 per cent, respectively), less rapid but still substantial in the Middle East and North Africa (–25 per cent) (Bongaarts and Watkins 1996). The major exception is sub-Saharan Africa, where at the national level there has been convincing evidence change in only a few countries, most in southern Africa: Zimbabwe, Botswana, and Kenya. In many other countries of sub-Saharan Africa, there is evidence of changed reproductive behaviour among some groups—not the aristocracies, as in Europe, but the 'new aristocracies'—educated urban professionals. If notions about diffusion are correct (there is some controversy, as elucidated in work by Philip Kreager 1996), this may spread rather rapidly to other groups in the population.

Many analysts, including myself, have concluded that the deliberate termination of childbearing before menopause was innovative reproductive behaviour, something new under the sun. In reaching this conclusion for the historical declines, we had to depend greatly on extrapolation from studies of local areas to national populations. For developing world declines, however, we have considerably more evidence: the alarm about population crisis, the development of survey techniques, and high-speed computing with which to analyse surveys, led to substantial and often quite well-funded efforts to measure fertility and contraceptive use in developing countries. From the earliest of these surveys in the 1950s and 1960s it was clear that few respondents were doing anything to control behaviour: they reported that they were not using either traditional methods of birth control or modern methods of family planning. By the latest round of these surveys in the late 1980s and the early 1990s, this had clearly changed: not only did very high proportions of respondents in most countries know about modern contraceptive methods, but substantial proportions in many countries were using them.

The research on historical fertility declines and on contemporary fertility declines that I have described had as their aims not only to describe fertility transitions but to understand the circumstances under which they occurred. By understanding, the researchers meant the specific type of understanding associated with positivist science. Both studies drew on contemporary theories of fertility change to formulate hypotheses and to collect data with which to test them. Although our theories are quite expansive about the determinants of fertility behaviour, in practice they emphasize the role of narrowly economic motivations for fertility control, measured rather crudely by levels of urbanization, education, female labour force participation, infant mortality, and so on. Attempts to explain fertility declines have not, however, been particularly successful. Fertility declines have occurred under a quite diverse set of conditions—fertility is now quite low not only in Europe but also in Taiwan, Kerala in India, and Costa Rica—and the variables used to test our hypotheses show only modest statistical correlations with women's childbearing and leave an unsatisfactorily large amount of unexplained variance (Knodel and van de Walle 1986; Cleland 1985). In all of these respects—the approach to explanation and the modest results—these two studies are quite similar to hundreds of other attempts to account for fertility transitions that have been mounted over the last three or four decades (for a review see Hirschman 1994).

These studies are similar in another way, and that is the absence of an explicit consideration of gender. The volume summarizing the results of the Princeton Project ran to some

449 pages. Yet the index of the summary volume, *The Decline of Fertility in Europe* (which I edited, Coale and Watkins 1986), has few references to women: there are twenty-one references to modernization and twenty-one to occupational differentials, but only five to 'women's status' and none to either men or sex (although there are seven references to abstinence). (To make matters worse, three out of the five references to women's status were in my concluding chapter, and deliberately inserted after the index was done when I realized that we had managed to write so much without mentioning women.) In Bongaarts and Watkins's analysis of developing world fertility declines, we used the UN's Human Development Index, a combination of apparently gender neutral indicators (industrialization, urbanization).

Yet there is a puzzle: what we are trying to explain in both projects are fertility rates based on data for women. In this sense, women are on virtually every page of these projects. In all respects except biology, men and women are considered interchangeable. Is this delicacy? A liberal commitment to a notion of a fundamental similarity between men and women? Or could it be that expectations of gendered behaviour are so taken for granted that they do not need to be made explicit?

To pursue this question further, I turn to a brief review of the way that expectations of gendered behaviour appear in our theories, sometimes explicitly, sometimes implicitly. Theories are of fundamental importance in empirical research on fertility change, for they determine the specific hypotheses that we test, they guide the collection of data, they shape our statistical analyses, and they help us to interpret our results. Our theoretical frameworks are built on maintained hypotheses, the assumed stories we tell about human behaviour that we do not test. These tell us not only what to 'see', but also what to ignore. We can find out whether the characteristics we expect to be important are indeed important: the problem is with what we ignore. If our theoretical frameworks lead us to expect gender to be unimportant, for example, we will not find out whether it is or not.

Gender in explanations of historical fertility declines

In examining gender in our theories, I will not say anything about the gender of the theorist, but rather focus on what appear to be shared notions of gender in the community of students of fertility change. I will begin with an example from reproductive biology. Neither men nor women are evident in the microscope of the scientists, only eggs and sperm. Yet in an article entitled, 'The Egg and the Sperm' and based on a review of textbooks on reproductive biology used in medical schools, Emily Martin (1991) shows us how even in the laboratory, white-coated scientists have used their imagination to tell gendered stories. The textbooks describe eggs as passive: they are 'transported', they are 'swept', or they 'drift'. In contrast, sperm are active: in the conventional story, multitudes of 'streamlined' sperm with 'strong tails' compete fiercely to burrow through the egg's coat and 'penetrate' it. Martin goes on to tell us that recent research has revised this romance. The egg is now given a more active role, the sperm presented as less competent than had been thought. In one study, the researchers discovered that the forward thrust of the sperm is extremely weak, and that their strongest tendency is to escape by attempting to pry themselves off the egg. If the egg did not trap the sperm and prevent their escape, few if any would reach the egg. Examining the language in which this research was published, however, Martin (p. 48) finds that: 'Even though each revisionist account gives the egg a larger and more active role, taken together they bring into play another cultural stereotype: woman as dangerous and aggressive threat'. The larger point she is making is that understandings of gender appear to be so profound that they even influence what we see in a microscope.

Fertility declines were produced by actual men and women, not eggs and sperm described as if they were women and men—drifting eggs and competitive sperm, or entrapping eggs and hapless sperm. It is thus even more likely that to explain fertility behaviour we would draw on what we know about men and women in the world around us. This is facilitated by a lack of knowledge about the way fertility declines occurred. This lack of knowledge about the way that women, men, or couples produced historical fertility changes is not surprising: although contemporary documents recorded the facts of birth rates, they did not record the motivations of those involved. Our ignorance about the way that women, men or couples produced the fertility declines in developing countries is more surprising, since we have had the opportunity to ask them about their motivations. That we have typically not done so is, I think, due to the preference of many contemporary analysts for a particular mode of scientific analysis, one in which we formulate theories that are expected to have universal applicability and then test them against data. Since positivists distrust what survey respondents say about their motivation, their values, their ideas, their attitudes, we prefer to assume their motivation in our theories, and then ask whether their behaviour corresponds to our imagining.

Although our theories are expected to be universally applicable, they are formulated by individuals living in particular times and places. To formulate our theories, we combine casual observation of the world in which we live with introspection—by which I mean that we ask ourselves: 'How would I behave in these circumstances?' If the experiences of groups of individuals are different, however, it is likely that their observation and their introspection will differ as well—a point that has been with respect to class by Marxist analysts, and with respect to gender by feminists (e.g. Hartsock's 1987 'standpoint' theory). Both men and women are active in population research. Yet it is fair to say that the theories of population change are associated with men: even in 1993, when 39 per cent of the members of the Population Association of America are women, and when 28 per cent of the articles published in its journal have at least one female author, the theories that guide our collection of data and its analysis and interpretation, are almost exclusively formulated by men.

It is easier to appreciate the extent to which notions of men and women influence our theories if we look at the accounts contemporaries gave of nineteenth-century fertility changes, since their views of gender are sufficiently different from our own in that they are usually more obvious. By the latter part of the nineteenth century, fertility declines were evident in western Europe. Contemporaries were quite aware of the enormous transformations associated with industrialization and its concomitants, such as urbanization, and it must have seemed reasonable to believe that these influenced fertility along with so much else. They also noted differential fertility: fertility appeared to be lower in urban than in rural areas, lower among professionals than among labourers.

In the latter part of the twentieth century, we view signs of fertility decline as something to be hailed, a sign that the 'population crisis' may be diminishing. This was not the case for most students of population in the nineteenth century. Fertility declines were evident first among what contemporaries considered the better sort of people, and raised the spectre of a change in the composition of the population: if the better sort of people were controlling their fertility but the others were not, it was feared that soon there would be too many of 'them'. Thus, there was rather intense interest in why some people were controlling fertility but others were not, and in what might be done about the situation. This interest led to the formation of eugenics associations, as well as to the implementation of policies driven by eugenic concerns (Barrett 1995; Hodgson and Watkins 1996).

Many nineteenth-century students of population blamed women, especially what they considered to be over-educated women, and women who had developed a taste for luxury.

Thus, the dour arch-conservative Spengler (in one of my favourite misogynistic quotes):

The arch-woman, the peasant woman, is a Mother. Her whole destiny desired from childhood, lies in this world. But now there is the Ibsen-woman, the comrade-wife, heroine of cosmopolitan liter-ature from nordic drama to Parisian novel. She has mental conflicts instead of children, marriage is a problem in Arts and Crafts, the main thing is 'to understand one another'. It does not matter whether an American lady cannot find sufficient reasons for having children, because she does not want to miss a single 'season', a Parisienne, because she fears her lover will leave her, or an Ibsen heroine, because 'her body belongs to herself'. They all belong to themselves, and are all infertile. (Spengler quoted in Eversley 1959: 161)

Other explanations were, on the surface, more gender neutral. Thus, Herbert Spencer thought that fertility was inversely related to civilization via physiology. A specialized and crowded society demanded a highly developed nervous system, which could only be achieved by draining the sub-stance necessary for generation (Eversley 1959: 188–9). Even this gender neutral formulation, however, lent itself to gender particular interpretations.

Many believed that the effects of civilization on generative ability were particularly deleterious to women. The leading authorities were not, as they are today, social scientists, but rather physicians. English physicians waded into the debate by drawing on their professional expertise. Physicians reported that: 'Modern females were indisputably more high strung and hysterial than their mothers and grandmothers', leading to an alarming increase in obstetrical problems (Soloway 1982: 146). An article in the *British Medical Journal* in 1904 claimed that the new woman was becoming mascu-line. 'She cycles, golfs, and plays hockey, and other sports, which increased her muscles while diminishing her pelvis' (Soloway 1982: 146). Soloway, writing of England, said that that the 'sexually rebellious, masculinizing tendencies of the women's movement particularly troubled doctors who

diagnosed it as a symptom of a deep disturbance in the "emotional nature" of the modern female. It was manifest in "atro-
phied maternal instinct, loss of femininity, and a lessened
development of "women's ways"' (Soloway 1982: 147).
Nineteenth-century England was presumably less patriarchal
than late twentieth-century western Kenya, which I will
discuss shortly, and the challenges to the nineteenth-century
order in England appear rather minor—cycling and hockey,
a demand for suffrage—compared to the more radical challenges to patriarchy by modern feminists. Nonetheless, mild
as these challenges appear in retrospect, they appear to have
made the doctors—presumably male—quite nervous.

Finding outrageously misogynistic statements by
nineteenth-century males (and some females) is absurdly
easy for those, such as myself, with late twentieth-century
feminist sensibilities. In addition, focusing on such statements
does not do justice to the earnest and often quite thoughtful
attempts of the many who commented on the issue in this
period. Much of the commentary focused not on biological
issues but on the social and, particularly, the economic basis
for restraints on fertility, both through delayed marriage (as
in the moral restraint of Malthus) and on the control of fertility within marriage (as among the Neo-Malthusians). An
important category of explanations for such restraints on fertility emphasized the role of the prospects of social mobility
offered by increasingly commercial and industrial societies.
The argument was that many children are an impediment to
social mobility, because of the expenses associated with their
rearing: thus, those who wish to rise on the social ladder—
what Dumont called 'social capillarity'—would deliberately
and voluntarily restraint their childbearing. It is harder to see
the role of gender in these arguments: they are often written
either without the personal pronouns that would indicate
gender, or they use the masculine pronoun, which at the time
could refer to men and women together as well as to men
alone. One would have to know more about nineteenth-
century society than I do to be sure, but I suspect that in

the context of nineteenth-century England, for example, women's avenues to social mobility consisted primarily in the choice of a marriage partner (as Trollope and other nineteenth-century authors made plain), whereas men's consisted both of marriage and their subsequent activities.

Instead of pursuing the gendered nature of explanations for population change in a historical setting, many of which, such as the effects of civilization on reproductive physiology, have been largely discredited (although there are residues in the concerns today of environmentalists about the effect of toxic chemicals on reproductive capacities), I now turn to the theories that have dominated our thinking about fertility declines. In modern times, the authority to pronounce on population issues has been largely taken from physicians and given to social scientists, particularly demographers typically located in university departments of sociology and economics. With few exceptions, our theories have put modern economics—by which I mean the kind of calculations that we believe those living in economically differentiated societies make—at the centre. The exceptions are amusing— a survey in Thailand, for example, that soberly asked the same questions about education and work of both men and women, but then asked women how often they went to the cinema, and asked men not about their movie-going experiences but the weightier question of whether they thought population growth was a problem in Thailand (Hogan and Frenzen 1981). Here, I suspect we hear the echoes of Spengler: women seduced away from their maternal responsibilities, not by nordic dramas or French novels, but by the silver screen—while men are worrying about serious issues such as the population explosion.

There are two major strands of explanation, one usually known as modernization theory, the other based on the neo-classical economic models of Becker and the Chicago School, often called the New Home Economics (NHE). The former is a capacious but often ill-defined approach to the societal transformations associated with industrialization and the spread of 'new ideas', whereas the NHE is focused more narrowly on a central set of issues that concern the efficient allocation of time and other resources, including those used to produce children, inside and outside the household (Becker 1981/1991). They have in common, however, their understandings of men and women. Both make assumptions about costs and benefits that are intuitively appealing: if children cost more and return less, it is sensible to think parents—perhaps men, perhaps women, perhaps couples—will want to have fewer of them.

In addition, and more centrally for the purposes of this essay, both frameworks present gender roles that hark back to the nineteenth-century notion of 'separate spheres'. Men work outside the home, whereas women are responsible for activities associated with the production of children and domestic services—a view that has considerable correspondence with what sources such as censuses and surveys tell us, or at least did until the massive increases in female labour force ˋparticipation. The doctrine of 'separate spheres' is reflected in the data and the form of our analyses. On the right-hand side of the equation we often find a woman's age, her parity, plus indicators that there is competition for her time and attention outside the home: her education and whether or not she works in the paid labour force. Husbands are rarely included in surveys, and information about husbands is often entirely absent, or limited to their education and occupation, asked of their wives. Although embedded in often highly complex statistical presentations, our analyses seem to assume that reproduction is the sphere of women, with men evident as shadowy figures who bring home the bacon but do little else. We do not ask much about women, to be sure—it is a short list of their characteristics that we imagine matter—but we ask even less about men (Watkins 1993).

The two approaches, modernization and the NHE, may be similar in their view of separate spheres, but they differ in their assumptions about the allocation of power within the household. (I say assumptions, because issues of power have been almost totally ignored until very recently.) In the modernization framework, the forces affecting behaviour are societal-level and impersonal—industrialization—even when the data concern individuals. Yet because women usually provide the dependent variable (e.g. birth rates, fertility preferences, contraceptive use) and because their characteristics either stand alone or predominate on the right-hand side of the equation, I think the implication is that women are in charge. The NHE is far less opaque about power. An 'altruist' is in charge, making decisions for other members of the family: the pronoun 'he' refers to the altruist, and 'she' refers to the beneficiary (Becker 1981/1991). Pollak (1985) describes the altruist as having the characteristics of a 'husband/father/dictator/patriarch' (see also Folbre, 1983). Thus, 'household demand' is his demand. In empirical practice, however, the distinction between the two approaches is diminished: both frameworks lead to the same gendered regression world where the characteristics of women predominate, and men bring home the bacon but do not do much else around the house.

The core issue in research in both frameworks is what leads women to abandon their domestic activities such that they delay marriage, do not marry at all, or bear fewer (or no) children. In both theoretical frameworks, the stories we tell emphasize activities that take them out of the household: as young girls to school, or as adult women to work. In the modernization framework, both men and women are expected to be influenced by their education, but the effects are expected to be quite different. If education leads a man to seek wider horizons, we do not typically assume that he will abandon his role as the family breadwinner, but we do assume that education will erode his wife's performance of her role. In the NHE, the effect of education is much simpler: it increases the amount the wife could earn if she were to produce for wages, thus raising the opportunity costs of her staying at home. The gap between the two theoretical frameworks is even less when we consider female labour force participation. In both, women's work outside the home is considered to compete with her domestic activities. Both also believe that work outside the home is likely to be more attractive than work inside the home: in modernization frameworks, there's a hint that staying at home all day is not so pleasant and women will leave it when they can, whereas in the NHE framework the issue is the wages for that work. The major theoretical difference is in who makes the decision, the woman herself (modernization theories), or the household despot acting on her behalf (NHE).

I think both theoretical frameworks reflect an understanding that pervades in the culture of population analysts: that women's commitment to the domestic sphere will continue only so long as she does not receive too much education or make a better deal for herself (or for the altruist) by working outside the family. The modernization approach has a clearer role for women: I believe we view women's commitment to the production of children and domestic services as rather fragile. When women become educated or work outside the home, we expect them to be less likely to marry, less likely to bear many children, and more likely to look for substitutes for breast-feeding. In this respect, we are perhaps not so different from Spengler. In the NHE approach, women do not seem to be so tempted—or, if they are, they remain firmly under the control of the head of the family firm.

Spengler, an arch-conservative, was dour about the consequences of teaching women to read—and perhaps more pessimistic than modern economists about the ability of men to control their women—because he thought declining fertility (particularly in some segments of the population) was a problem. In contrast, we interpret increasing levels of females' education as a sign of progress, liberating women from repetitive childbearing and domestic drudgery, and helping to solve the population crisis. Yet some ambivalence about this liberation, I believe, remains: Who will take care of the children? Who will cook dinner? Thus, although today's list of temptations for women is shorter and less misogynistic, I think the view that problems arise when women desert the domestic sphere is an enduring one in western culture.

Gender and population activists

Although I have said that there are similarities in the patterns of fertility decline in Europe and in the developing world, one substantial difference are the activities of population programmes. It has recently become fashionable in some academic circumstances to decentre our historical narratives, to make them less Euro-centric. The story of fertility decline is, however, one historical narrative that would be deformed if it did not privilege the role of western motivations and institutions. When it became evident that declines in mortality were not followed by declines in fertility, leading to rates of population growth that were high compared to those that had been known previously, there was considerable alarm. Demographers produced tables with projections showing that if current trends did not change, an increasing proportion of the population of the world would be those living in developing countries. The issue was not framed in the 'Us vs. Them' terms that the eugenicists had used earlier, but the sentiments appear similar, only cast in global rather than national terms. A book about the intensive efforts of international (but primarily western) family planning programmes was entitled *Nature Against Us* (Donaldson 1990): the photograph on the cover shows a group of women in saris. It does not require fancy deconstruction to draw the implication that women are associated with a teeming nature that needs to be controlled.

This alarm led to action in western countries (Hodgson and Watkins 1996). US foundations and other non-governmental organizations were in the lead (e.g. Ford and Rockefeller Foundations), followed by the aid agencies of national governments (e.g. USAID), and international institutions (e.g. the UNFPA). Oscar Harkavy, the long-time head of the Ford Foundation's population activities, describes the point when Ford decided to get involved in 1952. He quotes an unpublished oral history by the late Bernard Berelson, who then directed the Foundation's Behavioral Sciences Program

The Foundation got into population not because anybody saw this as a big emerging issue in the modern world, or anything like that. . . . The Foundation got into population because Rowan Gaither [an associate director, i.e. the vice president, of the Foundation] was looking for a subject matter that would attract the Board's support in the behavioral sciences, and he knew that two Board members were interested in population and they, so to speak, were interested in population because their wives were Planned Parenthood nuts and were always bugging them, 'Well, what are you doing about population?' And it had a concretness to it, and Rowan said, 'Let's do that. Let's have a study. Let's see what we can do about population'.   (Harkavy 1995: 10)

Subsequently, Ford manoeuvred to stimulate invitations to establish family planning programmes in developing countries. A good example is India. Douglas Ensminger (the first of the Ford Foundation's overseas representatives) met with the Health Minister, who had previously refused to take an interest in family planning. He urged her

to consider the effect of India's population growth on the very poor and the need to assist those who wanted help in limiting their fertility. The Minister then requested Ensminger to bring to India someone who could advise her on a policy statement on family planning. Ensminger asked her to put the request in writing, and she did so.   (Harkavy 1995: 132)

At its height in 1966–7, the operational style of the New Delhi office is described by Harkavy as 'remarkable for its expansiveness'. It was staffed by seventy-two expatriate professionals and an administrative and technical corps of 177 Indian nationals, sixty-three other full-time employees, plus sixteen foreign employees of institutions supported by the Foundation to conduct programme activities in India.[3] Many of the expatriates were assigned to ministries and field projects, 'offering hands-on technical assistance, and in many cases actually operating programs and projects'. (Harkavy 1995: 130). Although New Delhi was the site of the largest such operation, it was certainly not the only one: by the early 1960s, the Population Council (with support from Ford) dispatched representatives to establish family planning programmes in Taiwan, South Korea, Turkey, Tunisia, Thailand, and Kenya, among other developing nations (Harkavy 1995: 43).

How we got from 'two planned parenthood nuts' to the point where there was an enormous bureaucracy devoted to population control and with a budget of about four to five million dollars in 1994 (Parker Mauldin, pers. comm.) would surely be a fascinating study. Part of the story has been told, both by those who support its aims (Piotrow 1973; Donaldson 1990) and those who do not (Warwick 1982; Maas 1972), and some of its elements are clear (Hodgson and Watkins 1996). Pressure from private organizations, in a climate of widespread public concern about the 'population crisis'—stimulated in part by the writings of scientists funded by Ford and Rockefeller Foundations and by the Population Council (itself funded by these foundations), led to involvement of the US government and USAID, which in turn was crucial in persuading the UN to set up a specialized agency, the UNFPA, for population matters.

As we have seen, pressure was brought to bear, and developing countries by the dozens adopted family planning policies linking population and development (Barrett 1995).

---

[3] 'To house the New Delhi staff, Ensminger had constructed a magnificent campus including a strikingly handsome office building and a guest house resembling a small modern hotel with its own swimming pool, all set in a green oasis of carefully tended lawns and sparkling fountains. Early each morning, before embarking on his strenuous working day, Ensminger would arrive in a black victoria drawn by two black horses, take a salute from the Indian guards and inspect the premises.' (Harkavy 1995: 131)

Although the initial formulation of this linkage had been that development would automatically induce population change (based on the modernization theories we have just considered), by the 1960s this had been reversed: development, it was believed, would be severely constrained by rapid population growth. At an international meeting on population matters in Bucharest in 1974, there was considerable objection by developing countries who argued that what they needed was aid in economic development, not aid in controlling their population. By the subsequent international conference in Mexico City in 1984, many countries had capitulated, signing on to a population policy that was virtually identical across most countries (Barrett 1995: 247) and receiving foreign funds to support the establishment of family planning clinics and the distribution of modern contraceptives.[4]

One result was the establishment of national councils to promote family planning, for example through posters and radio shows. A second and important result was the expansion of family planning programmes on the ground: typically integrated into maternal and child health clinics, these programmes dramatically increased the accessibility of modern contraceptives for those who wished to use them.

Understandings of gender are either explicit or not far beneath the surface of the population control movement, a point that was increasingly appreciated by feminists and other women's advocates, and made public in the most recent of these international population meetings in Cairo in 1994 (McIntosh and Finkle 1995). I have already pointed to the

[4] India was the first country to adopt a policy, in 1952. By 1970, 26 developing countries had population control policies or programmes, and 22 provided support but had no explicit policies; by 1991, the number of countries that officially endorsed comprehensive population policies reached 69 (Barrett 1995: 249). The timing of the adoption of such policies was statistically associated with characteristics of the individual country, such as their gross domestic product and their rate of population growth. It was also, however, statistically associated with the extent of their involvement in the international community, as measured by signing the 1966 UN declaration on population, and participation in major international conferences on population between 1946 and 1991 (Barrett 1995: ch. 10).

title of a recent book, *Nature Against Us*, where Nature is visually depicted as female. In an introduction to a special issue of the journal *Demography* in 1968, devoted to family planning programmes, an article by Harkavy and others attributes the progress of family planning programmes to 'men and money'. Editor Donald Bogue uses military metaphors: the family planning movement is an 'organized protest' and a 'large-scale action'; its efforts are of 'truly heroic proportions', a 'crusade', a 'Holy War'; the articles in this issue are an array of "battlefront reports" (Bogue 1968: 539–40). Some of the problems cited in this issue are due to inadequate government support, religious opposition, and so on, but others are due to the difficulty of persuading audiences to use modern contraceptives ('insufficient penetration of the audience'; Wilder and Tyagi 1968: 774). Who was this audience that was insufficiently penetrated? Although the rhetoric often speaks of 'persons' or 'couples', it is clear that the focus is on women's responsibility rather than men's in solving the global problem of uncontrolled population growth.

How did it come to be that women were targeted, that family planning programmes were placed in 'women's spaces', maternal and child health clinics? As far as I can tell, there was little debate about targeting women rather than men, or even couples. In an article on family planning among the rural poor in the United States, the author says: 'Family planning in the United States to date has been confined largely to women. This makes sense in the same way that the concentration of programs in urban areas makes sense' (Wilber 1968: 909).

My point here is not that these prior discussions which ultimately targeted women (rather than men or couples) were necessarily ill-advised, but that they were based on our understandings of gender differences. In the 1960s, before I went to graduate school, I participated in some of these discussions as a volunteer in the first family planning programme in the Dominican Republic and later as a volunteer for Planned Parenthood in Washington, DC. It seemed entirely appropriate to me that these efforts were aimed at women. My friends and I believed that women had more reason than men to be concerned with the consequences of childbearing, and we took it for granted that their husbands simply would not cooperate. The family planning activists were, I suspect, no different.

We have evidence that people often believe differences between males and females to be far greater then they really are (Bleier 1987; Epstein 1988; Marini, 1990). Some of the evidence available at the time that family planning programmes were being implemented in developing countries shows that men may have been motivated as strongly as women to limit family size, or even more so. For example, Dow (1967) found that about 40 per cent of urban Kenyan males reported no 'best thing' or particular good attached to large family size, compared to 29 per cent of their wives. Caldwell (1968: table 2) found similar results for Ghanian urban elite males and females, and for males and females in Lagos. Moreover, Caldwell's (1968) analysis of a variety of surveys showed little difference between the percentage of males and of females who stated 'contraception is right' or 'contraception is wrong' (table 9); among the Ghanian elite, in Lagos, and in an all-India survey, more males than females expressed interest or willingness to use family planning (Caldwell 1968: table 11; Poffenberger 1968; see also Roberts *et al.* 1965). This evidence, however, was ignored.

Perhaps the decision to target women was a legacy of the birth control movement in the west, which also focused on women (Hodgson 1991): both Margaret Sanger in the United States and Marie Stopes in England directed their attention to women (Seccombe 1992). Also, it may be that evidence from surveys, even if correct (there is some distrust of their results), was fundamentally irrelevant; other considerations properly may have carried more weight. These include the more rapid development of coitus-independent techniques of contraception for women (although we might ask why this

35

was the case) and the availability of an infrastructure of maternal and child health clinics. Or, possibly, demographers as well as funders may have concluded rightly that leaders in the developing world were reluctant to target men, or local clinic workers may have drawn on their knowledge of gender relations in their own society to conclude that husbands would simply not cooperate. Nonetheless, the lack of explicit justification for focusing on women as targets of these programmes, and the disregard of survey evidence, lead me to conclude that this focus almost certainly was influenced by unsupported assumptions about differences between men and women in their willingness to use modern contraceptives.

It should be noted, however, that the population control movement shows, at times, a considerable ambivalence about the women who are their targets. On the one hand, women are often depicted as apathetic, mired in traditional cultures that prevent them from acting rationally and in their own best interests. On the other hand, women are seen to be the only hope: if anyone is going to save us from overpopulation it is the women.

Gender and fertility change in Kenya

I have talked about the boardrooms of large foundations where men debate the population crisis and what needs to be done about it; now I will turn to the reaction of men and women in four small areas of Kenya.

The following research project was stimulated by the mounting evidence that our theories were not as fully supported by the data as we had expected, by unexpected patterns in these data, and by reflections on my own experience as a mother. What the stories of calculations of the cost and benefits left out, I recognized, was the potential of social interaction to contribute to social change (Watkins 1995). The theories based on modernization usually treat countries as if they were isolated; those based on NHE have, as Paul David has pointed out, treated families as islands (David 1985). Drawing on my own experience, my formulation was of a world that was more crowded and noisy, and was gendered: I recalled gossiping with other women during my child-rearing years about deliveries that were hard or easy, about babies that slept too little or vomited too much, about husbands who did not help enough with the cooking, about the high cost of raising children these days, about our wanting to earn money. When we initially explained our project to the Kenyan interviewers as women's gossip, they giggled; when we said we were also interested in men's gossip, they looked startled, and said 'men don't gossip'. As we will see below, men chat and gossip with each other too, although in Kenya what they told us that they say to each other about family size and contraception is somewhat different from what women told us they say to each other.

One of our research sites is on Mfangano Island in Lake Victoria—a five-hour trip over reasonable roads to the district capital of Homa Bay, then a two-hour trip over dreadful roads to a small port, then two hours in a boat. For westerners, this island is a picture-book place with steep hills and tumbling greenery, mud huts with thatched roofs, no roads, no electricity, no post office, women washing clothes in the sparkling lake. It appeared quite remote to our Kenyan colleagues as well—one asked whether those on the island voted, another, when she first saw the island, said 'You'd know you were in Africa, but you wouldn't know where'. Yet even here, when Luo women were asked: 'Could you tell us about the last conversation you had about family planning?', they responded with something like: 'Oh, it was last Thursday when some of us were going to the lake to bathe, and my friend Phoebe said "Its such a burden taking care of children these days, I don't want to have more", but Mary said that "Some say what if you have only a few and they all die?" Or "Jennifer told me that Martha had gone for family planning, but Jennifer said she wouldn't do that, because Rose had done it and she was sick for a long time afterwards".'

Despite the poverty and remoteness, then, the people of these areas are actively debating fertility decline. Many outside the area believe that Kenyan men and women would be better off with fewer children. In the mid 1980s, Kenya was a poster-child of population crisis propaganda: it had one of the highest growth rates in the world, a rate that implied doubling in less than twenty years. By 1993, Kenya was being held up as a positive model to other sub-Saharan countries, an example of what can be done in a context of limited economic development. A national survey showed that fertility had fallen from an average of seven per woman to an average of five, and that a third of the married women of reproductive age were using birth control, most of it modern (Kenya, 1994). Indeed, in some areas of Kenya, rates of contraceptive use are about as high as in developed countries. In rural South Nyanza where we were working, however, there has been much less change: six children is considered a small family, and about 11 per cent are using contraception (Kenya 1994). Yet both women and men are intrigued by what appear to them as new ideas and new possibilities, and I have no doubt that the Luo areas that we studied are going to experience a substantial transformation in reproductive behaviour in the next decade. Nonetheless, as far as they are concerned, the issue is still open—very open.

In our research, we took two approaches to trying to understand what might accompany reproductive change in these areas. One was a set of long interviews in June and July 1994, with a representative sample of 40 women and 40 men, in which we asked them about recent conversations they had had about what we called 'the goodness or badness or large or small families', and recent conversations about methods of family planning. We also conducted eight focus groups. The other approach was a conventional survey, conducted in December 1994 and January 1995, with a representative sample of approximately 800 women and 800 men, in which we asked primarily about their networks—with whom they had talked and when.

What are they saying to each other? Just as the western theorists expected, they are concerned about the economic costs and benefits of children. But whereas western theorists, influenced by Adam Smith, apparently think that these costs and benefits are based on individual circumstances and readily calculable, such does not seem to be the case here, as the following quotation from a focus group of women age thirty to thirty-nine indicates

Moderator: 'Sometimes people say that having many children is better than having few, while others say that few children is good.'

FGW: 'Many children is a good thing when there is some work to be done. Say I have four and you have two, my work will be done faster than yours.'

FGW: 'But when it comes to food, the one with two children eats better than the one with four children.'

FGW: 'Many children is hard, but looking after few children is easy, so few children is good. I have realized that I am one "leading" here with children [she has more than the others]. I must say the truth—if I compare the way I had children sometime back in early 1982, it feels different now. Looking after them now is different from 1982. Now, even if the source of income is high it is different. Even if one has, say, two children and the source of income is very little, looking after them is not easy. When one has enough food to feed them on, looking after children is not a problem, and even there being many is not noticed. Once they have food, clothing is secondary, isn't it?'

F: 'But you see the world of today, we don't just think of food, there is education, and secondary education is around 10,000 shillings. Say the person with two children, [the two children] are sent away from school because of the lack of school fees, this person would be able to take her children back to school before me, even if it is taking one at a go. That is when one should give the children spacing, [so that] when one is in standard one, another one is in standard five. So then there is space, when one is going to do Form Four, the next one is in Form One.'

Here, one woman begins by presenting an argument for many children, that many children contribute more to the family economy. The next responds with another category of expenses, food, in which having many children is a disadvantage, and dismisses the category of clothing costs. Then the others add yet other category, the costs of education. In the conversation, they also formulate a model of the consequences of socio-economic change: In the past, food may have been the predominant concern, but things have changed and there is now education to consider. Later in the focus group, the women (unprompted) consider other categories of costs and benefits: some might want many children because of the risk of mortality; many noisy children might lead the husband to stray; if both parents die it is easier to find new parents for a small number of children than for eight; there are more 'wants' in the Kenya of today than in the past, prices in the past were 'fairer' than prices today. In effect, the women are estimating prices and what economists call 'equations of motion', the link between an action or choice made at one time and the distribution of possible consequences (Montgomery and Casterline 1996). In circumstances of imperfect information and strong uncertainty, it seems plausible that individuals would consider relevant not only their own circumstances, but would also do as they are doing in the focus group above: increasing the evidence available to them by discussing with others in similar circumstances the relevant categories of costs and benefits, and the appropriate weights to be assigned to each.

This segment of a focus group is rather uniform in presenting arguments for fewer children. This was not always the case, however, and it was evident that community opinion was mixed, and individual women and men ambivalent.

Perhaps because our research team was associated with the family planning programme, objections to its goals were often couched in the words of others, 'some say that . . .', as in the following quote from a woman in a focus group

The famine was so severe that people who had many children found it very tough. There was a young boy who passed by where we were waiting to be collected to come here, so I imagined that people who have boys of that size must be finding it rough feeding them during the famine. Two kilograms of flour is nothing to them. Still, some people say that having many children is a good thing, especially when it comes to work like weeding. Large families are able to weed their farms within a short time.

Men also discuss the economic costs and benefits of children with each other. They differ somewhat, however, both in the list of costs and benefits, and in the importance they give them. Men are more likely to emphasize the monetary costs of children that are considered to be men's responsibilities: school fees, clothing, medical expenses. The primary forms of non-monetary wealth, land and cattle, are owned by men not women. In addition, men are expected to have more opportunities to earn money, since they are expected to participate more than women in the modern economy.

The differences in men and women's motivation for wanting more or fewer children diverge to a greater extent when we consider motivations that are not easily translated into monetary terms, and not captured by our conventional explanations for fertility change. Men add to the list of motivations concerns about the continuation of their lineage. Luo society is patrilineal and polygynous, and traditionally it was the aim of each man to have as many wives and children as possible, to continue their lineage. Several men also added voting power—if the Luos continue to have many children, they will be more successful in the democratic competition than ethnic groups considered to be their rivals for government money. Women sometimes repeat these concerns, although they are usually bracketed as 'some say . . .', again suggesting a distance from these opinions, perhaps because the government is considered to be an affair of men.

To a much greater degree than men, women talked about ordinary life with small children, such as a woman who said 'I didn't like the idea of this child is crying here, another one urinating there', or another who said 'You can be just giving birth, so that you cannot even leave the door, you are too occupied with the child that you cannot even go to the market'. (The market is a source of small income, but it is also a major locus of sociability.) A few talked about the inability to wear fashionable clothing if they are always pregnant or breastfeeding. Although fashion may appear trivial to some, compared to the cash costs of children, fashion is a way of expressing a sense of self, of personal and also of group identity, and that as such it is not trivial—and it did not appear trivial to some women. A segment in a focus group of women aged thirty to thirty-nine nicely combines both economic and non-economic considerations.

FGW: 'Yes, we do hear people talking about family planning [in English]. I would like to space my children, for example getting another baby four years after this one [referring to a baby in her arms]'. I also want to put on the fashions that other women put on. You cannot live by changing from a big stomach to breastfeeding all the years through.'

Moderator: 'You cannot put on any fashion now?'

FGW: 'You cannot, because after giving birth, whenever you are recovering, there is always another pregnancy on the way even before recovering from the previous one.'

FGW: 'When the people begin to start coming [for visits after the birth], you are already heavy with another pregnancy.'

FGW: 'We [women] are in a big problem, because when

you give birth, you are washing blood (sanitary towels) cleaning children who have excreted all over.'

[Later in the same focus group]:

Moderator: 'Why do you think women turn to these things [family planning methods] after marriage?'

FGW: 'I think after having children they begin to experience problems in the house, then they turn to those methods.'

Moderator: 'What are those problems that they experience?'

FGW: 'When there is not enough money to feed the children, clothe them, she cannot pay their school fees. Life changes immediately when children arrive. A woman realizes that she cannot dress well as she used to—she can only afford second hand clothes, she cannot even buy soap for bathing. These are the problems that force a woman to begin "family planning" [in English].'

Although men in these areas of Kenya are responsibile for the economic support of children, particularly monetary expenses such as school fees, clothing, and medicine, women often consider the economic support of children their responsibility as well. The non-economic costs, however, are seen as specifically female concerns. As one woman in a focus group said 'Many children is a big problem. Men do not know this problem because he leaves the house in the morning, he goes to walk and comes back in the evening everyday. It is the woman whom the children scream at, one minute this one is crying here, another one has excreted there'. Another woman in the focus group proceeded to elaborate and agree: 'Children are given by God to us mothers, having many children is not the best. Sometimes you are hungry, children are screaming for food at the top of their voices, but the man is not at home to stand all this'. The women we interviewed appear to have a notion of separate spheres, much as our theories depict: what becomes striking, however, is the absence of noise and vomiting children in the theorists' version of the domestic sphere, but its importance to these Kenyan women.[5]

It is these burdens of ordinary life, both economic and non-economic, that I believe lead women to evade men's power and use contraception without the knowledge of their husbands. Luo society is patriarchal: men trade cattle for women, and are expected by other men as well as by women to be the ultimate decision-maker. When we asked men and women who made decisions about family planning, they invariably answered 'The men do'. To our surprise, however, a substantial proportion added something like 'But if he doesn't agree you just use your brain', or 'But after all, it's the woman who must decide because the children are her burden', going on to tell us how women can hide pills in the thatch of the roof, or in the flour in the kitchen (men are not supposed to enter the kitchen). Although our theories may envision an orderly gender system, the women are disorderly. The women we interviewed do not use the 'rights' language of the Enlightenment or of the Cairo conference, and would not agree with the feminist slogan, 'Our bodies, our selves'. Rather, they justify the secret use of contraception in terms of their daily lives, of women's burdens, which they say are different from men's.

To use contraception secretly is a direct subversion of traditional gender relations in this community, and both men and women are quite aware of it. Indeed, the men are quite nervous about it. Our local interviewers were secondary school graduates, and both men and women expressed, to us, full agreement with the goals of Kenya's national family program—indeed, they even regurgitated program propa-

---

[5] It is worth noting that these types of non-economic concerns do not appear to be specific to women in South Nyanza: similar comments can be found in reports from quite different areas of the world. Thus, Mita and Simmons (1995: 8) report women talking about the advantages of fewer children in terms of dressing nicely, and quote one woman as saying 'More children make so much noise and disturbance to the mother, it is unbearable. This one does not have cloth, that one wants food, another one is sick, and arranging marriage is also a tough thing'. (See also Watkins and Danzi 1995; Garey 1987.)

44

ganda, telling us how families with only a few children are wealthier and happier than those with many children. When we asked some male interviewers what men said to each other about the secret use of contraception, however, we got quite a different response: a vehement disapproval of such behaviour. 'They say that "Women who are secretly using have no right to decide what to do in the house, if I discourage this she should stick to my discouragement, not take some tablets with my not knowing it, if I find this out I'll beat her"' (Tom S. and Tom M., Owich).

Husbands are concerned that wives may use contraception secretly to indulge in extramarital affairs, or to go on a 'birth strike', risking his hopes for a lineage. They are even more concerned, I believe, at the challenge to male power. As I noted earlier, there is some suggestion that nineteenth-century students of population were concerned about such challenges: the women who cycled and played hockey, thus improving their muscles but destroying their pelvises. Given the available methods of family planning in the nineteenth century—some mix of abortion, abstinence, and withdrawal—it may have been somewhat more attractive for women who wanted to space their children or stop childbearing to convert their husbands than to turn to abortion, the only method under their control. In Nyanza Province, I believe that most women would still prefer to convert their husband—'you try to explain it to him, little by little'. If he still refuses, however, both men and women understand that the alternative—using modern methods of contraception secretly—is quite accessible.

Conclusions

The nearly worldwide declines of fertility that I began by describing represent a major social change, the consequence of altered reproductive behaviour. Begun in most countries of Europe and European settlement in the latter part of the nineteenth century, it is playing out now on beautiful Mfangano Island in Lake Victoria, as it is in developing countries. I have discussed three sets of actors in this drama: the theorists who have guided our research on the causes of fertility decline, the programme activists who have guided our interventions in the developing world, and the men and women of Nyanza province, Kenya, who are currently debating among themselves whether lower fertility is a good thing or not. The first two believe they know something about why these changes have occurred, the latter are, I believe, in the process of enacting them.

For none of these sets of actors is the process of change in reproductive behaviour gender-neutral; all draw on their understandings of different motivations and behavior of men and women. Scientists, especially those of a positivist persuasion, tend, I believe, to distrust individual experience and subjectivity. We thus expend a great deal of effort to protect ourselves: rules of science provide elaborate procedures to guard against subjectivity, enforced by all sorts of professional apparatus such as peer review. Nonetheless, it would appear to be quite difficult to control our tendency to see the world in images of males and females drawn from our experience in our own society, even when we are examining 'passive' eggs and 'competitive' sperm in a microscope.

Thus, it is perhaps not so surprising that theorists draw on their own experiences, they write male and female roles rather differently. For Spengler, as we have seen, it is women who are responsible for the troubling differentials in fertility between rich and poor: the rich women prefer novels to children, while the poor keep breeding, a class version of 'nature against us'. For the modernization theorists, it is steam engines or the silver screen that tempt women to evade their domestic responsibilities, while men continue to bring home the bacon or discuss the population problems that face the nation. The story is somewhat different again for the neo-classical economists: here it is women's time that is usually at issue rather than anything as frivolous as the cinema, but men are in charge, allocating responsibilities in accord with economic efficiency. For the population activists, it is 'men and money' who will lead the charge against their targets—the women who are their despair as well as the only hope of population redemption.

In closing, let me turn once more to science which, after all, is the theme of the Herbert Spencer Lectures in this as in other years. Modern feminists have claimed that 'the personal is political', scientists, especially those of a positivist persuasion, distrust both. Those who attended the Spencer Lectures in 1982, on science and politics, may recall Professor Margaret Gowing's lecture. In it, she argued that 'an old and constant theme about the relationship of science and politics . . . that science is pure and politics is dirty' (Gowing 1984: 53). She goes on to use the post-war story of scientists and nuclear weapons to conclude that the scientists 'turned out to be, indeed, remarkably like the politicians'. I believe the stories in this essay demonstrate that we have done no better at keeping the personal out of the science of population change. By personal, I mean here our understandings of gender, the way we look at 'passive' eggs and 'competitive' sperm.

Does the fact that the theories we use to understand population change or the programmes we use to intervene in reproductive behaviour are suffused with a social construction of gender matter? I think it does. Positivists acknowledge that theories can come from personal experience, introspection or intuition. But these should not, positivists believe, influence our evaluation of the empirical evidence. We are sufficiently worried that they will because we erect elaborate procedural bulwarks against the influence of experience and subjectivity on our evaluation of empirical evidence, bulwarks that have become firmer with the professionalization of science. I have not talked today about the way that gender might influence our evaluation of evidence, not because I do not think it happens, but because I think the more interesting issue is the extent to which our understanding of gender have influenced our theories.

Our theories have not, I believed, guided us very success-fully in understanding the pervasive and rapid fertility declines. We certainly have very good descriptions of fertility change, and I believe we know considerably more about why fertility declined than did the analysts of the nineteenth century. Our empirical work has indeed helped us understand one domain of human behaviour, the domain that consists of a calculus of the narrowly economic costs and benefits of chil-dren. As we have done this, however, we have confined women to the domestic sphere, and cast a discreet veil over the activities within it. The failure to consider something as apparently trivial as 'women's gossip' is a mistake, as is our evident discomfort with those crying babies. In this, we are perhaps not so different from the Luo men, who 'discuss' rather than 'gossip', and who, their wives claim, 'aren't there to hear because they are out walking around'.

A more general implication is that we should be more attentive to the fit between gender as it is constructed in our theories and gender as it is constructed in the societies we study. Relaxing the reins on our curiosity—stepping outside our local cultures to observe the interactions of men and women—can surely provide us with information that other-wise we might miss, about those whose experience of the social construction of gender may be quite different from our own.

Were gender only present in the formulation of our theo-ries, perhaps whether or not we get the story straight would not be very consequential outside the halls of academe. Yet western understandings of gender also inform the population control movement, which has brought modern contraception to places as remote as Mfangano Island. Population activists have make it possible for women to get packets of con-traceptive pills or injections of Depo-Provera provided by western donors and distributed in maternal and child health clinics. Although a few programmes have been coercive, for many women and many men in many countries these pro-grammes have, I believe, offered them opportunities which they appear to have been eager to grasp. In addition, family planning programmes have provided opportunities for women to subvert a traditional gender order that would not have been otherwise available. That this challenge to male power can be successfully implemented, and perhaps even mounted, is due to the gendered construction of developing world populations by family planning programmes initiated in the west and implemented by national governments. This has been welcomed by some of the women we interviewed in Kenya—but it has certainly disturbed some men.

REFERENCES

BARRETT, D. A. (1995). 'Reproducing Persons as a Global Concern: The Making of an Institution'. Unpublished doctoral dissertation, Department of Sociology, Stanford University.

BECKER, G. S. (1981/1991). *Treatise on the Family*. Cambridge, MA: Harvard University Press.

BLEIER, R. (1987). 'Science and Belief: A Polemic on Sex Differences Research'. In *The Impact of Feminist Research in the Academy*, ed. Christie Farnham. Bloomington, IN: Indiana University Press, 111–30.

BOGUE, D. J. (1968). 'Progress and Problems of World Fertility Control'. *Demography*, 5: 539–40.

BONGAARTS J. and MENKEN, J. (1983). 'The Supply of Children: A Critical Essay'. In *Determinants of Fertility in Developing Countries*, ed. R. Bulatao and R. Lee. New York: Academic Press, 27–60.

——and WATKINS, S. C. (1996). 'Social Interactions and Contemporary Fertility Declines'. *Population and Development Review*, 22: 639–82.

CALDWELL, J. C. (1968). 'The Control of Family Size in Tropical Africa'. *Demography*, 5: 598–619.

CLELAND, J. (1985). 'Marital Fertility Decline in Developing Countries: Theories and the Evidence'. In *Reproductive Change in Developing Countries*, ed. John Cleland and John Hobcraft. Oxford University Press, 223–49.

COALE, A. J. (1986). 'The Decline of Fertility in Europe since the Eighteenth Century as a Chapter in Human Demographic History'. In *The Decline of Fertility in Europe*, ed. Ansley J. Coale and Susan Cotts Watkins. Princeton, NJ: Princeton University Press, 1–30.

——and WATKINS, S. C. (eds.) (1986). *The Decline of Fertility in Europe*, Princeton, NJ: Princeton University Press.

DAVID, P. (1985). 'Comment on Gary S. Becker and Robert J. Barrow, "Altruism and the Economic Theory of Fertility"'. In *Below-Replacement Fertility in Industrial Societies: Causes, Consequences, Policies*, ed. K. Davis, M. Bernstam and R. Ricardo-Campbell. *Population and Development Review*, **12**(Suppl.): 77–86.

DONALDSON, P. J. (1990). *Nature Against Us: The United States and the World Population Crisis, 1965–1980*. Chapel Hill, NC: University of North Carolina Press.

DOW, T. C. Jr. (1967). 'Attitudes Towards Family Size and Family Planning in Nairobi'. *Demography*, **4**: 780–97.

EPSTEIN, C. F. (1988). *Deceptive Distinctions: Sex, Gender and the Social Order*. New Haven, CT: Yale University Press.

EVERSLEY, D. E. C. (1959). *Social Theories of Fertility and the Malthusian Debate*. Oxford: Clarendon Press.

FOLBRE, N. (1983). 'Of Patriarchy Born: The Political Economy of Fertility Decisions'. *Feminist Studies*, **9**: 261–84.

GAREY, A. I. (1987). 'Fertility on the Frontier: Bringing Women Back In.' *Nineteenth-Century Contexts*, **11**: 63–83.

GOWING, M. (1984). 'An Old and Intimate Relationship'. In *Science and Politics: The Herbert Spencer Lectures 1982*, ed. Vernon Bogdanor. Oxford: Clarendon Press, 52–69.

GUINNANE, T. W., OKUN, B. S., and TRUSSELL, J. (1994). 'What Do We Know about the Timing of Fertility Transitions in Europe?' *Demography*, **31**: 1–20.

HARKAVY, O. (1995). *Curbing Population Growth: An Insider's Perspective on the Population Movement*. New York: Plenum.

HARTSOCK, N. (1987). 'The Feminist Standpoint: Developing the Ground for a Specifically Feminist Historical Materialism'. In *Feminism and Methodology*, ed. Susan Harding. Bloomington, IN: Indiana University Press, 157–80.

HENRY, L. (1961). 'Some Data on Natural Fertility'. *Eugenic Quarterly*, **8**: 81–91.

HIRSCHMAN, C. (1994). 'Why Fertility Changes'. *Annual Review of Sociology*, **20**: 203–33.

HODGSON, D. (1991). 'Ideological Origins of the Population Association of America'. *Population Development Review*, **17**: 1–34.

——and WATKINS, S. C. (1996). 'Population Controllers and Feminists: Strange Bedmates at Cairo?' Unpublished paper.

HOGAN, D. P. and FRENZEN, P. D. (1981). 'Antecedents to Contraceptive Innovation: Evidence from Rural Northern Thailand'. *Demography*, **18**: 597–614.

KENYA (1994). *Kenya Demographic and Health Survey, 1993.* Calverton, MD: National Council on Population and Development, Central Bureau of Statistics and Macro International.

KNODEL, J. (1983). 'Natural Fertility: Age Patterns, Levels and Trends'. In *Determinants of Fertility in Developing Countries: A Summary of Knowledge*, ed. R. Bulatao and R. D. Lee. New York: National Academy Press, 61–102.

——and VAN DE WALLE, E. (1986). 'Lessons from the Past: Policy Implications of Historical Fertility Studies'. In *The Decline of Fertility in Europe*, ed. Ansley J. Coale and Susan Cotts Watkins. Princeton, NJ: Princeton University Press, 390–419.

KREAGER, P. (1996). 'The Limits of Diffusionism'. In *The Methods and Uses of Anthropological Demography*, ed. Alaka Basu and Peter Aaby. Oxford: Oxford University Press.

MARINI, M. M. (1990). 'Sex and Gender: What Do We Know?' *Sociological Forum*, **5**: 95–120.

MARTIN, E. (1991). 'The Egg and the Sperm: How Science Has Constructed a Romance Based on Stereotypical Male–Female Roles'. *Signs*, **16**: 485–501.

MASS, B. (1972). *Population Target: The Political Economy of Population Control in Latin America.* Montreal: Editions Latin America.

MCINTOSH, C. A. and FINKLE, J. L. (1995). 'The Cairo Conference on Population and Development'. *Population and Development Review*, **21**: 223–60.

MITA, R. and SIMMONS, R. (1995). 'Diffusion of the Culture of Contraception: Program Effects on Young Women in Bangladesh'. *Studies in Family Planning*, **26**: 1–13.

MONTGOMERY, M. R. and CASTERLINE, J. B. (1996). 'Social Learning, Social Influence, and New Models of Fertility,' in *Fertility in the United States: New Patterns, New Theories*, eds. J. B. Casterline,

R. D. Lee and K. A. Foote. A supplement to *Population and Development Review*, Vol. **22**: 151–75.

PIOTROW, P. T. (1973). *World Population Crisis: The United States Response*. New York: Praeger.

POFFENBERGER, T. (1968). 'Motivational Aspects of Resistance to Family Planning in an Indian Village'. *Demography*, **5**: 757–72.

POLLAK, R. A. (1985). 'A Transaction Cost Approach to Families and Households'. *Journal of Economic Literature*, **23**: 581–608.

ROBERTS, B. J., YAUKEY, D., GRIFFITHS, W., CLARK, E. W., SHAFIULLAH, A. B. M., and HUQ, R. (1965). 'Family Planning Survey In Dacca, East Pakistan'. *Demography*, **2**: 74–96.

SECCOMBE, W. (1992). 'Men's "Marital Rights" and Women's "Wifely Duties": Changing Conjugal Relations in the Fertility Decline'. In *The European Experience of Declining Fertility, 1850–1970: The Quiet Revolution*, ed. J. R. Gillis, L. A. Thilly, and D. Levine. Cambridge, MA: Blackwell, 66–84.

SOLOWAY, R. A. (1982). *Birth Control and the Population Question in England, 1877–1930*. Chapel Hill, NC: University of North Carolina Press.

UNITED NATIONS (1995). *World Population Prospects: The 1994 Revision*. New York: United Nations.

WARWICK, D. P. (1982). *Bitter Pills: Population Policies and Their Implementation in Eight Developing Countries*. Cambridge, UK: Cambridge University Press.

WATKINS, S. C. (1986). 'Conclusions'. In *The Decline of Fertility in Europe*, ed. Ansley J. Coale and Susan Cotts Watkins. Princeton, NJ: Princeton University Press, 420–50.

——(1987). 'The Fertility Transition: Europe and the Third World Compared'. *Sociological Forum*, **2**: 645–73.

——(1993). 'If All We Knew About Women Was What We Read in Demography, What Would We Know?' *Demography*, **30**: 551–77.

——(1995). 'Social Networks and Social Science History'. *Social Science History*, **19**: 295–311.

——and DANZI, A. (1995). 'Women's Gossip Networks and Social Change: Childbirth and Fertility Control Among Italian and Jewish Women in the United States, 1920–1940'. *Gender and Society*, **9**: 469–90.

WILBER, G. (1968). 'Fertility and the Need for Family Planning Among the Rural Poor in the United States'. *Demography*, **5**: 894–909.

WILDER, F. and TYAGI, D. K. (1968). 'India's New Departures in Mass Motivation for Fertility Control'. *Demography*, **5**: 773–9.

WILMOTH, J. R. and BALL, P. B. (1992). 'The Population Debate in American Popular Magazines, 1946–1990'. *Population and Development Review*, **18**: 631–68.

WILSON, C. (1984). 'Natural Fertility in Pre-industrial England, 1600–1799'. *Population Studies*, **38**: 225–40.

WRIGLEY, E. A. and SCHOFIELD, R. S. (1983). 'English Population History from Family Reconstitution: Summary Results 1600–1799'. *Population Studies*, **37**: 157–84.

3

Sexual Differentiation and Cognitive Function

LUCIA JACOBS

In 1588, Michel de Montaigne concluded, 'I say that male and female are cast in the same mold: save for education and custom the difference between them is not great' [62]. If Montaigne could be asked about the relative properties of men and women in the area not only of morphology and outward behaviour, but also of cognition I suspect he would give the same answer, perhaps more adamantly. Yet it is an interesting question: how do the sexes differ in their perception and processing of information about their external world? And if such differences exist, do they develop due to 'education and custom', or are cognitive sex differences a consequence of sexual differentiation? And if such differences exist, can we suppose that they are functional (i.e. do they occur in other species and have they arisen through processes of natural selection?).

Questions about sex, gender, and cognitive ability are topics of intrinsic and universal interest, a field of enquiry which has generated tens of thousands of scholarly articles. It is also a field mined with potential political dangers and divisions, and one into which biology ventures at great risk. The firm establishment of the principles and ramifications of

I would like to thank Kim Beeman, Marc Breedlove, John Dark, Kate Onstott, Stephanie Preston, Margo, Wilson, and Carol Worthman for helpful discussion of the ideas discussed here. I would also like to acknowledge the financial support of the University of California at Berkeley.

sexual differences, unrelated to cultural context, is an important goal, but it lies on the far side of treacherous intellectual terrain. But we can, at this juncture of the expedition, find places to set our feet that will not lead to disaster, generalizations that, presumptuous though they may be, biologists feel will survive their time and their cultural context. For example, I would argue that it is a landscape that must be understood within a historical framework, which, to a biologist, is the framework of evolution by natural selection. Despite the controversy, all would agree that we have at least three good landmarks on which to base our map. These are: first, that in all vertebrate species, male and female cognitive abilities and brains are more alike than different; second, that such differences can arise through the action of hormones on neural development; and third, that the internal environment of the hormonal milieu is influenced both by the genetics of sex determination and by the external environment. Hence, sex differences in the brain and in cognitive abilities can be strongly influenced by the combined actions of the environment and an individual's genetic make-up.

Using these landmarks, each discipline constructs its own map of this terrain, each perhaps with a distinctive distortion, much as Saul Steinberg's 1975 'View of the World from 9th Avenue' is a topologically correct but geometrically distorted representation of the world from the point of view of a New Yorker [73]. My route through this terrain is based on the map of a cognitive psychologist trained in the practice of ethology and the theory of evolution. I begin with the biological underpinnings: the distribution of cognitive sex differences in species other than our own, and the causes and consequences of this pattern in other species.

The puzzle underlying cognitive sex differences is why such a fundamental trait as cognition should differ between the sexes. Yet the same can be said of even more fundamental traits, such as body size. For example, in many polygynous mammals, despite similarities in ecological niche between males and females, males are larger than females [4]. The functional explanation for this sexual dimorphism is that in polygynous species, males compete amongst themselves for access to females, and therefore require proportionately larger body sizes than females in order to reproduce. In the red deer (*Cervus elaphus*), for example, larger stags are more successful in defending a harem of hinds and hence a stag's body size is directly proportional to his reproductive success [17].

Sexual selection and song

Sexual dimorphisms in body size or antler weight may have little to do with cognition, but illustrate the adaptive significance of sex differences. The boldest and most easily explained example of a cognitive sex difference is also found in the context of males competing for female mates. This is the ability of songbirds, also known as passerine birds, to learn their species-specific song. Passerine birds comprise over half of all bird species in the world, and in many species males must learn to sing [57]. These song-learning species show much variability in the timing and tutoring of song; some species learn only at one time period during development (critical period or age-limited learners) and some learn throughout life (open-ended learners), some learn from a parent and some learn from surrounding adults. Yet across all song learning species, there is a sex difference: males sing more complex songs than females. Although it is true that in some species females and males sing duets, where each part is of equal complexity, in no species do females learn to sing more complex songs than males [76].

The function of this distinct sex difference is clear: males require learned song to attract female mates and to compete against male rivals. The ability to learn song is thus subject to sexual selection, the selective pressure which result from competition among individuals of the same sex [76]. Song learning ability lends an advantage both in territory disputes and in female preference: in open-ended learners, males with large song repertoires attract more females. A large repertoire is also necessary for effective territory defence, because in many species, the mode of competition among males is their ability to match the songs of their rivals. Neighbouring males mimic each other's repertoire, song for song, apparently an efficient method by which they size up each other's repertoire [8]. Since repertoire often increases with age, this may provide the listening bird with some estimate of the competitive characteristics of his neighbour.

For these and other reasons, birdsong is considered a sexually selected trait, with advantage accruing to those who can learn more complex song than rivals. And since in most species, it is the males who compete more strongly than females for mating opportunities, it is the males who receive the brunt of the sexual selection for song learning. And hence the clear dimorphism in learning ability.

How this dimorphism develops and by what precise mechanism this occurs, is itself a thriving scientific discipline [6]. In brief, however, it is a story of hormonal environments, created by the hormone output of the fetal and perinatal gonad. If the brain tissue of the developing songbird, such as the well-studied canary or zebra finch, experiences high levels of the hormone that normally emanates from the male gonad, during the critical period immediately after hatching, this leads to the structural enhancement of certain nuclei, known as the song nuclei. In the zebra finch, where females do not sing at all, this produces a striking difference in morphology between male and female brains. The male brain contains a series of interconnected nuclei, the song nuclei, which are necessary to learn and produce song and which are smaller or absent in the female brain. The detailed circuitry and functions of these nuclei is outside the province of this essay; the obvious conclusion, however, is that both learning ability and its underlying brain structure are sexually dimorphic [6].

Hence, here is an everyday occurrence of a sexually dimorphic learning ability, with underlying dimorphism in its neural basis. The different hormonal milieu of males and females produce sex differences throughout the fine structure of these brain areas (e.g. the volume of brain regions, the number of neurons, the size of neuronal cell bodies, the length of dendrites, and the distribution of receptors for steroid hormones). Yet if hatchling females are injected with the steroid hormone oestrogen, the volume of song nuclei areas are increased via reduced neuronal death and such females will both sing and learn song syllables from a tutor. If these females continue to receive male-appropriate steroid hormones as an adult, she will develop further changes in structure, all with the effect of producing a female brain whose song nuclei are increasingly similar to those of males [6].

Although birdsong is a clear example of a cognitive sex difference in vertebrates and an excellent system for the study of their development, it also has the drawback of the special case; no other species, avian or otherwise, learn songs. But in its general outlines, it can be thought of as a template to search for other cases of sex differences, with these attributes: it shows enhanced development in the sex experiencing greater sexual selection, it is shaped by the hormonal environment during a critical perinatal period, and with the degree of neural dimorphism is directly related to the degree of cognitive dimorphism. These attributes are present only in one example of cognitive function in mammals and this is in the realm of spatial cognition.

Sexual selection and space

Spatial cognition is usually defined to include assorted perceptual and mnemonic abilities, such as the ability to perceive and locate visual objects in space and the ability to create map-like internal representations of the environment. Thus 'spatial cognition' includes both simple and complex spatial processing.

Male and female laboratory rats, the domestic strain of the wild Norwegian rat (*Rattus norvegicus*), show striking differences in what they remember from exploring new environments. These differences emerge when the rats are asked to use visual landmarks to return to the food they had found earlier, such as location of bait in a maze [92]. How well males and females are able to find the bait depends on how the visual appearance of the test room has been changed. If the maze is surrounded by a white curtain, so that the shape of the space is changed, males make many more mistakes. It is as if they are using the shape of the room as a compass, to tell them where they are. Thus, if the room is rectangular with a door at one end, the male rat can place himself in this simple map, and remember, for example, that he has already looked for bait at the 'door end'. Or he can use several of these far-off landmarks, such as the door, or the corners of the room, at the same time, to define (or triangulate) a specific point in the room, such as the arm of a maze. Thus, if the male is paying most of his attention to these types of far-off landmarks, he will be badly handicapped if these outer landmarks are suddenly covered by a curtain. This is exactly what happens: he starts looking in the wrong places, revisiting places where he has already eaten the bait, for example, until the curtain is once again removed. Then he can once again solve the maze with almost no errors.

Female rats behave quite differently. They also appear to learn the corners of the room because they also make more mistakes when the curtains are used. But they are not as affected as the males. This is because females have also paid attention to the location of objects that are closer to the maze, such as items on the table or glued to the wall. The females not only use the compass and triangulation technique to define a place in space, but also remember the items that were near that place, such as the box on the table that was behind that arm of the maze. If these objects are rotated, females rotate their search pattern, just as if the whole room had been rotated. A male, however, would continue to use the far-off landmarks and would therefore not change his search strategy at all. If the objects are not just rotated but are mixed up, so that different objects are exchanged with each other, then females suddenly can no longer find the bait in the maze; she now makes as many mistakes as the males surrounded by the curtain.

What is the mechanism by which this remarkable cognitive sex difference arises? Once again, it is the early hormonal environment [92]. If a rat, regardless of sex, experiences its first week of life in the presence of a certain level of reproductive hormone (oestrogen) in its blood, either produced naturally by male testes or artificially by injection, then that individual, as an adult, will pay attention to the 'compass marks' or distant landmarks, and it will make many more errors in the curtained maze. If a rat does not experience this level of oestrogen, either because its brain produces a certain protein which mops up excess oestrogen, as happens in normally developing females, or because disease or experimental intervention prevent the testes from producing testosterone (which is then converted to oestrogen, the necessary form of hormone), then the rat will pay attention both to distant corners and closer objects, as described for normal females.

This scenario is almost identical to that described for the development of birdsong. This is perhaps surprising that such different learning abilities, song and space, would develop in such similar ways: after birth or hatching, and in response simply to the hormones produced by the neonatal gonad. We can only speculate why this is so; why perhaps sophisticated learning abilities only appear late in brain development, after the staples of sensory perception, motor coordination, learning, and memory of sensory information have already been built. Perhaps, too, it is a good thing to have this tardy development of these structures, so that they develop not as a closed genetic programme, but as one more flexible and responsive to the environment.

Moreover, if spatial learning parallels bird song learning,

then it should also be mediated by a part of the brain that develops during the critical postnatal period and that is responsive to gonadal hormones during this time. These conditions are met by one structure, the hippocampus. The hippocampus is a large forebrain structure with both general and specific cognitive functions. Its general function is the ability to construct and remember conceptual relationships between events [27]. It also has a specialized function to solve problems of spatial representations, such as the ability to map and construct novel routes in the external world [67]. Moreover, like song nuclei, the hippocampus may be sexually dimorphic in size in both birds [78] and mammals [42]. In laboratory rodents, the hippocampus is sexually dimorphic, with a male advantage, in cell number [94], in the volume of fibre tracts [55], and in the volume of the certain dendritic arbors [47]. And, just as in birdsong nuclei, these sex differences can be manipulated by changing the early hormonal environment in which the hippocampus develops; females treated with testosterone at birth show a masculinized pattern of spatial learning and hippocampal structure [72]. Thus, both sex differences in spatial learning in the rodent and sex differences in the hippocampus can be altered with hormones, although the precise mechanism by which hormones change the fate and structure of the hippocampus is not fully understood.

While it is clear that male birds sing so that females will be attracted to them, it is not at all clear why male rats should navigate based on the shape of a room; at least, when the question is stated in that way. So we must instead step back and ask: what is the function of navigation, under natural conditions? Why would males and females differ in how they accomplish this? The answer lies in the observation of space use in nature. Sex differences in maze navigation have been demonstrated in several species of wild rodents. In all of these species, males and females have different patterns of natural space use: males use large, undefended areas which encompass the territories of several females, which live in small, defended spaces. This sex difference in space use arises from different mating strategies of males and females: females defend an area large enough to feed themselves and their offspring, while males spend their time searching for females receptive to mating. Under this polygynous system, the difference in natural spatial movements by males and females is reflected in similar differences in spatial learning, such as maze performance. That this difference is related to space use is suggested by the further observation that in monogamous species of rodents, where males and females use territories of the same size, there are no sex differences in the number of errors made learning mazes [32, 33].

Thus, sex differences in behaviour are directly related to learning spatial information in nature. How could this explain why male laboratory rats concentrate on the corners of the room? Perhaps it is because males specialize in learning to find locations quickly, by triangulating their coordinates from distant objects. This is an extremely efficient way to solve a maze which only requires a simple solution, such as learning the location of a few bait locations. But this strategy yields little other information. Females, in contrast, may be learning their territory in much greater detail. Hence, females appear to solve the maze more slowly only because they take in more information than do males. Thus, if females learn two types of spatial information (e.g. both compass direction and the individual features of different landmarks), their progress must be slower; they are learning more and hence learn more slowly [93]. Again, this makes good sense in the real world: female rodents rear litters by their own efforts, and should know their own territory well in order to forage more efficiently. In contrast, for males to increase their success as reproductive citizens, they must travel farther, encounter, and court a greater number of females.

The advantage of spatial navigation ability in males has been best demonstrated in field studies of the thirteen-lined ground squirrel (*Spermophilus tridecemlineatus*). In this species, females are receptive for only one day per year.

Males arrive on a receptive female's territory and follow a queuing convention; the first ones to arrive are also the first ones to mate. A male's ability to find receptive females as soon as possible on their day of oestrus thus has a direct effect on a male's success [75].

Thus, like songbirds, rodents also show cognitive sex differences. The direction of the sex difference is not fixed, but varies predictably with mating system, and these patterns predict sex differences in the hippocampus, a major neural substrate for spatial navigation. Finally, the sex-specific spatial specializations appear to be adaptive solutions to the different spatial problems faced by males and females of these polygamous species in nature.

Yet, compared to the magnitude of cognitive and neural sex differences in songbirds, these differences are not great. In this sense, Montaigne was still correct in saying that even for rodents, males and females are more alike than different.

Of mice and men

For the animal shall not be measured by man. In a world older and more complete than ours they move finished and complete, gifted with extensions of the senses we have lost or never attained, living by voices we shall never hear. They are not brethren, they are not underlings; they are other nations, caught with ourselves in the net of life and time, fellow prisoners of the splendour and travail of the earth.   Henry Beston (1928) [11]

Yet even sovereign nations may obey the same natural laws. We are mammals, after all, and show typical mammalian sex differences in body size. Sexual dimorphisms in structure are common; in fact, whenever one sex cannot maintain exclusive access to another, the tools of competition, such as weapons, body size, even testes size, appear in more exaggerated forms. The degree of sexual selection determines both the trait and the degree to which the trait is sexually dimorphic. For example, highly polygynous male primates have larger testes and canines than males from species where polygyny is less extreme [4, 18].

Patterns of mate competition also predict the magnitude of sex differences in the brain [43]. The dimorphism of song nuclei, for example, is greater in the zebra finch (*Poephila guttata*), where females do not sing at all, than in the canary (*Serinus canarius*), where females sing a simple song. The sex difference in song nuclei size is even smaller in the bay-breasted wren (*Thryothorus nigricapillus*), where mated pairs sing intricate duets, composed of two equally complex parts. Hence the larger the sex difference in song complexity, the larger the sex difference in song nuclei [16].

Sex differences in hippocampal size also vary with natural patterns of learning ability and space use. In contrast to poly-gynous vole species, in the monogamous pine vole (*Microtus pinetorum*), where a male, under natural conditions, uses the same size territory as his mate, there is no sex difference in either spatial learning ability or hippocampal size [32, 44]. The same pattern is seen in the space use patterns of birds: in the brood parasitic brown-headed cowbird (*Molothrus ater*), females compete for suitable host nests in which to lay their eggs. Because they must lay their unwelcome egg without being detected by the host, females must remember both the locations of host nests and their hosts' laying schedule to execute a successful foray. In the North American cowbird, this behaviour is correlated with a female advantage in hip-pocampal size [78]. In Argentinean cowbirds (*M. bonariensis*, *M. rufoaxillaris*, *M. badius*), the degree to which any species relies on brood parasitism determines the size and direction of this female advantage in hippocampal size; species where the male and female search for host nests together show a smaller female advantage [71].

Thus the degree of investment in structures needed to compete for mates is correlated with the level of mate com-petition. In primates, this can be predicted from the number of females to whom a male is able to maintain exclusive access, and sexual dimorphism in body size in primates is directly related to the ratio of females per male in a social unit [18]. Because human polygyny is characterized by a relatively small number of women per polygynous group, sex differences in stature and other measures should be correspondingly small, at least in comparison to species where the ratio of available females to available males is much smaller. In accordance with this prediction based on our degree of polygyny, we humans show sex differences in stature that vary between 4 and 10 per cent among cultures [31]; in contrast, the Northern elephant seal (*Mirounga angustirostris*) male, who can maintain exclusive access to a large harem of females, may weigh three times as much as an adult female [4].

Hence, similar body size in men and women already suggests that there are only small socioecological differences between them and that sex differences in cognitive or neural sex differences might also be small or insignificant. Such differences are indeed small [20]. They can also be elusive, varying from study to study. Only too often the conclusion reached by a series of studies on a particular trait is that the magnitude of the difference is slight and sensitive to experimental conditions. Perhaps fuelled both by this uncertainty and the universal interest and importance of the issue, hundreds of researchers have studied the effect of sex on cognitive ability [53, 54]. In recent summaries of this contentious literature, few cognitive measures show a strong effect size (defined as the number of standard deviations between group means). Yet because of the importance of the question (i.e. whether men and women differ in intellectual ability), I concur with Sandra Witelson's conclusion: 'Although they have little, if any, practical significance for any individual, such differences may have major theoretical significance' [95].

Sex differences in human cognition

Sitting in my office in Tolman Hall, I am reminded that before discussing data on humans, I can do no better than to quote

Edward C. Tolman himself, who attempted a similar synthesis on mice and men with his 1948 paper, 'Cognitive Maps in Rats and Men'—'My argument will be brief, cavalier, and dogmatic. For I am not myself a clinician or social psychologist. What I am going to say must be considered, therefore, simply as in the nature of a rat psychologist's ratiocinations offered free' [85]. Keeping in mind, then, that the differences are small, how do men and women differ in cognitive ability?

Women excel in tasks requiring forms of fluency, or what might be described as a rapid deployment of attention and skill. For example, the largest female advantage is seen in 'motoric fluency', where fine motor skills must be used to place pegs into holes, or objects must be constructed by putting things together in a specified order. Verbal fluency, such as the ability to list words beginning with a prescribed letter, also shows a female advantage [20]. Finally, women outperform men on tasks requiring 'attentional fluency': the ability to identify rapidly similarities or differences between objects, match objects by their similarities, or find one symbol amid distractors. Mathematical differences, such as the solutions to algebraic equations, can also be calculated more quickly by women than by men [51].

Perhaps akin to 'attentional fluency' is a woman's ability to unconsciously notice and remember the locations of objects, and to recognize, more quickly than men, that an object has been moved or taken away. When college students are asked to study a drawing of a random array of common or unfamiliar objects, women remember the locations more accurately. Women also remember the locations of objects in a room in which they were asked to wait briefly [26, 80]. It is as if women are keeping a continuous record of the visual images in their environment. This is also seen when they are moving around in space; in either tabletop or full-size spatial mazes, where a route must be traced or walked between two points, women are more likely than men to remember the landmarks en route to the goal [30, 51], similar to the female laboratory rats, noticing and remembering more details about their environment.

The female advantage is, however, never large. Large cognitive sex differences are found only in spatial tasks with a male advantage. The most consistent task to show this male advantage is the Shepard–Metzgar mental rotation test, where one compares and matches three-dimensional objects by mentally rotating the novel object into the same orientation as the sample [41]. For cognitive sex differences, these are large effects [20]; although, to put these differences into perspective, sex differences in height show effect sizes that are twice as large as those seen on mental rotation, which shows the largest effect size in a human cognitive sex difference [34].

Just as women seem to excel in noticing many things and changing their attention quickly, men seem to excel at tasks with the opposite requirement: those that require the single-minded pursuit of a goal that involves the representation of direction. For example, men throw projectiles much more accurately than women, although there are no sex differences in the ability to block the same projectile [89]. Men learn maze routes more quickly and with fewer errors than women, and can reverse directions on the maze with fewer errors, although they remember fewer details about the route they have taken. This also appears to be a spatial representation based on compass direction, rather than route finding in relation both to landmarks and compass direction as in women [30]. Again, this sex difference in cognitive style is remarkably reminiscent of that observed in male laboratory rats, who prefer to orient to distant cues offering direction information rather than deducing their location from the array of visible landmarks at their current vantage point [92].

Thus, similar to results from rodent studies, men and women differ most consistently in spatial tasks, and do so because they solve the problem in different ways. In the task of mental rotation, the type of strategy used, whether a purely visuospatial strategy or by verbal coding of the objects, can be detected by imposing an intervening distractor task. Because processing capacity is limited, two tasks that use the same resources interfere with each other, and hence performance on either task declines. On average, a woman's performance declines if she must solve an irrelevant verbal (but not spatial) task and the opposite is true of men, whose performance is affected only by intervening spatial tasks [14].

Development and differentiation

Cognitive systems in birds and rodents are critically tied to the posthatch or postbirth interval; experimental manipulations of the developmental hormonal environment demonstrate that sexual differentiation of song learning and spatial learning are due to the action of steroid hormones, and hence are a consequence of genetic and gonadal sex determination. Thus the development and differentiation of cognitive sex differences suggest that the underlying mechanism is similar in these two types of learning.

The similarities in the use of spatial strategies by male and female mammals (at least, in rats and humans) suggest that spatial ability in humans might also be organized by perinatal hormones. This question has been addressed with data from situations where disease, pathology, or abnormal genotype have produced abnormal hormonal environments in the developing human [20].

For example, in the case of girls with congenital adrenal hyperplasia, the adrenal glands, which normally produce low levels of androgen, produce excessive androgens prenatally. Because aromatase enzymes in the brain can convert androgens to oestrogens, increasing the level of either steroid hormone can masculinize neural substrates; it simply depends on the type of steroid receptor expressed by the structure. Because these androgens masculinize the external genitalia, these girls can be recognized at birth and successfully treated, limiting the excess androgen exposure to periods before and

just after birth. Hence, cognitive abilities that are masculinized in these girls must be due to the effect of excess androgens on neural substrates that differentiate during this
period. One consequence of this condition is an increase in
performance on spatial tasks such as mental rotation,
although there is no affect on verbal intelligence [20].

In contrast, girls with Turner's syndrome have lower than
normal oestrogen levels due to a chromosomal abnormality
(XO genotype). As adults, they show cognitive deficits both
in verbal fluency and in spatial visualization [66]. Because
they seem to be handicapped in a diverse group of tasks, it
has been suggested that their deficit can be defined as 'processing speed and attention' [20]. In other words, perhaps
they lack precisely that attentional and perceptual fluency
which characterizes a woman with normal development.

Spatial deficits can also be found in men with patho-
logically low levels of androgens during development, such
as in idiopathic hypogonadotrophic hypogonadism. Here, the
testes fail to be sufficiently stimulated to produce normal
levels of androgens. It is not clear exactly whether the androgen deficits occur pre- or postnatally, however, males with this
condition have significantly impaired spatial ability [37].

It thus appears that in humans, as in the laboratory rodent,
it is not the genetic sex of the individual that determines
spatial ability, but its hormonal environment during development. However, developmental trajectories in the brain are
profoundly influenced by the relative time period spent at
each developmental stage [29]. To understand the sexual differentiation of the brain, we must know both which hormones
play an active role and when they produce their effects. For
example, both congenital adrenal hyperplasia and Turner's
syndrome result in increased levels of steroid hormones
before and after birth; both show predictable effects on
spatial cognition. However, an excess of hormone that is
administered before birth only does not appear to affect
spatial cognitive abilities. This was concluded from studies of
girls whose mothers were treated with a synthetic oestrogen

(diethylstilbestrol or DES) to maintain pregnancy and hence exposure was limited to the prenatal period. Girls exposed to this oestrogen showed normal spatial ability and levels of aggression, two factors which generally show the greatest degree of sexual dimorphism, although they did show a more masculine pattern of language lateralization [20]. Thus, spatial and verbal cognitive traits appear to differentiate at different periods in development. Prenatal hormones may thus influence language lateralization but abnormal hormone levels must continue into postnatal life to influence the differentiation of spatial abilities. This may be similar to the pattern seen in rodents, where spatial learning in females is influenced both by pre- and postnatal oestrogen levels, whereas the male strategy of spatial learning is influenced only by the postnatal hormonal environment [92].

Sex differences in the brain

The evidence for an underlying neural basis for cognitive sex differences in humans is controversial [15, 20]. There must be at least three reasons for this: first, as in cognitive traits, only small or inconsistent differences would be predicted. Second, our species is characterized by plasticity, with an extended period of development; this, too, should affect the development of cognitive abilities. Third, the tasks where men and women differ may call on more generalized cognitive abilities than those described in songbirds and rodents. If we cannot map a cognitive trait to a specialized structure (e.g. a song nucleus) but must map it instead to a constellation of multi-purpose brain structures (and even a seemingly specialized structure such as the hippocampus has more identified functions in humans than the rat [52]), then, once again, we should not expect to find strong sex differences in any one structure.

Thus it should not come as a surprise that men and women appear to differ most not in the size of a particular brain structure but in a fundamental feature of brain organization: the degree of lateralization. The average adult female brain appears to be more symmetrical and hence less lateralized than the male brain [60]. The consequences of symmetry for brain function are seen in the relative robustness of the female brain in response to stroke; being less lateralized and hence with brain function redundantly represented, women recover speech more quickly after trauma to the left hemisphere [51]. Female brains are less lateralized than male brains even on listening tasks, such as the accuracy with which the time of sound arrival is judged in each ear (the dichotic listening task). Men show hemispheric specialization in this task, with a stronger right ear (i.e. left hemisphere) advantage than do women [39]. More recent examples have used brain imaging techniques to compare the lateralization of language function in men and women. Once again, the female brain is fundamentally more symmetrical, using both frontal cortices to solve a verbal task such as rhyming; the male brain uses predominantly the left hemisphere during the same task [77].

A symmetrical brain requires a greater coordination of effort to process simultaneously information in both hemispheres. Hence, the pathways connecting the cerebral hemispheres should be more extensive in the symmetrical brain. For example, both men and women who represent speech primarily in the right hemisphere have a significantly larger corpus callosum, the main fibre tract connecting the left and right cerebral hemispheres, than people who represent speech in the left hemisphere only [70]. This suggests that bilateral representation of function, whether in males or females, is related to the size of fibre tracts connecting the two sides of the brain.

However, on average, the size of these commissures should be larger in women than in men. There seems to be some evidence for this in three large fibre tracts that connect left to right cerebra in humans. The anterior commissure, a fibre tract connecting left and right temporal neocortices (the area of neocortex in the vicinity of one's ears) is larger in women than men [1]. Another sex difference is found in the massa intermedia, a tract connecting subcortical areas in the thalamus. This odd structure, present in other primate species but often not found in humans at all, is more likely to be absent in men than in women, and when present, it is smaller in men than in women [1].

However, the most consistent and well-studied sex difference in commissural volume is found in the corpus callosum. Specifically, the difference appears in the posterior callosum, in an area called the splenium, with female splenia having greater maximal length, greater area as a function of brain weight, and greater total callosal area [23]. This result has been controversial; because of the importance of this fibre tract, this result has been replicated by many researchers; those using exactly the same methods as the original study have found the same or a smaller female advantage, although those using other methods have found no difference [20]. The same pattern has also been described in rats: the splenium of the corpus callosum is larger in females than males [46].

The development of lateralized function

How do such sex differences in laterality differentiate? If laterality is associated with differences in cognitive ability, which are themselves strongly influenced by perinatal hormones, then brain laterality may also be hormonally mediated.

Evidence from songbirds and laboratory rodents suggest that steroid hormones do influence the development of sex differences in lateralization of brain structure and function. For example, the male canary's song production is severely disrupted by severing the left, but not the right, nerve which innervates the syrinx [69]. Male gerbils (*Rodentia: Meriones unguiculatus*) show structural asymmetry in the brain nucleus involved in their ultrasonic courtship call, which is larger in

73

the left than right hemispheres; more important, the development of this lateralization depends on the presence of testosterone [40]. Finally, there are more generalized effects of steroid hormones on lateralization of structure or function: female rats exposed to postnatal androgens show a masculinized pattern of lateralized movements [24, 92].

Similar effects may be found in humans, although the data must be interpreted cautiously. One example is lateralization of function in women with low oestrogen levels: Turner's syndrome women show even less lateralization of function in the dichotic listening test than do normal women [68], suggesting that a certain level of steroid hormone is required for normal lateralization to develop. Other evidence comes from measures of lateralization and cognitive function in male and female homosexuals. Because homosexuals are similar to their opposite sex in sexual orientation, one might expect cognitive similarities as well, if such traits have a common developmental origin. Some studies have found that gay men score lower than heterosexual men on spatial tests [74]. Gay men also show less cerebral lateralization than heterosexual men, since the size of the anterior commissure is larger in gay than heterosexual men [2]. In addition, homosexuals show different patterns of functional laterality on dichotic listening tasks: neither gay men nor lesbians show the widely replicated pattern of perceptual asymmetry with consistent right-handedness. In other words, being right-handed predicts a strong right ear bias in heterosexuals but not homosexuals [58]. All of this is consistent with the idea that hormones, development, and degree of cerebral laterality are somehow inextricably linked.

Laterality and rates of development

The male and female mammal (at least in laboratory rodents and humans) thus appear to differ most dramatically in the domain of spatial cognition. These cognitive sex differences are related to a general difference in cerebral symmetry: the male brain tends to be more asymmetric than the female brain, which correlates with smaller volume of interhemispheric commissures. Such structural differences are determined not by genetic sex but by the postnatal hormonal environment; experimental manipulations or hormonal abnormalities or perhaps sexual orientation are associated with predictable shifts in the degree of lateralization and spatial ability.

Why should perinatal hormones cause such a shift, increasing or decreasing the degree of symmetry in the developing brain? Perhaps for two reasons: first, the brain does not grow symmetrically; and second, because the brain grows asymmetrically, the length of the developmental period profoundly affects the degree of cerebral asymmetry.

One of the first hypotheses that development is often inherently asymmetric derives from the observation that the left and right sides of a developing embryo responded differently to experimental manipulations, suggesting that some cytoplasmic factor appears to be responsible for the formation of an innate left and right side (described in Morgan [63]). In 1978, Michael Corballis and Michael Morgan proposed a new theory of brain lateralization based on this idea [22, 64]. Arguing that all growth is asymmetrical due to innate properties of the egg's cytoplasm, they proposed that this asymmetry also shows an innate bias for the left side to precede the development of the right side. Eventually, the right side of the brain, given enough developmental time, may catch up with the left and produce a symmetrical structure. But should development continue further, the right may surpass the left and a right bias could eventually develop. Hence, the longer the development, the more potential for asymmetry exists, and the more lopsided a brain might become, as seen in our own species, the 'lopsided ape' [21]. Subsequent researchers have improved on this theory; for example, Ursula Mittwoch has suggested that maturational gradients may start with the left but then switch to the right.

Thus, in any structure the direction of asymmetry should be predictable from its developmental age, relative to other structures. Waves of development proceed down the body, head to toe, and the longer a structure has been differentiated, the greater the probability that its asymmetry will have proceeded from left-biased to right and then back to left, explaining, for example, why arms and legs show different patterns of lateralization [61].

Yet even this model may be too simple. In her 'growth vector' hypothesis, Catherine Best incorporates not only left–right differences, but also anterior–posterior and dorsal–ventral vectors. In the human brain: 'The overall effect on the hemispheres is as though some force had twisted the left hemisphere rearward and dorsal, while twisting the right hemisphere forward and ventral'. The result of these onto-genetic contortions is a different allotment of tissue to the two hemispheres, with a concomitant change in commissural volume to accommodate the coordination of two, more symmetrical and hence more equal hemispheres. And because brain structures develop in a rough phylogenetic order, with 'primitive' areas, such as primary sensory and motor areas developing before areas that associate these inputs, Best hypothesized that such tertiary association areas should develop last in the right hemisphere. Therefore, an increased developmental period should be associated with enhanced higher functions of the right hemisphere, such as visuospatial functions [10].

In accordance with this hypothesis, it appears that the rate of maturation may indeed predict traits associated with symmetry: the degree of cerebral asymmetry, the volume of the cerebral commissures and the level of spatial ability. Once again, there is evidence from humans with chromosomal abnormalities. Turner's syndrome women (XO genotype) show an increased prenatal development rate, and this is associated with greater cerebral symmetry and poorer spatial ability than women with a normal XX geno-type. In contrast, men with supernumerary-X syndrome (XXX or XXY genotype), experience higher than normal steroid hormone levels, develop more slowly than the normal XY genotype men, and have lower verbal abilities relative to spatial abilities [10].

These are the extremes, however. If the growth vector hypothesis is correct, then normal sex differences in spatial ability could be a manifestation of the growth rates of men and women which produce differential growth of the cerebral hemispheres and hence differences in laterality. If so, then an individual's rate of maturation should predict the differentiation of late developing structures and hence their level of spatial cognition.

In 1976, Deborah Waber found that sex differences in spatial ability were a consequence of sex differences in age at puberty; late-maturing girls showed superior spatial ability. Thus, the difference between boys and girls could be ascribed not to sex but to age at puberty and it appeared that cognitive sex differences were a result not of sex but of maturation rate, which, on average, is associated with sex [88]. Her initial finding was based on girls from extremes of the maturation distribution; subsequent attempts at replication failed when such extreme maturation groups were not used. However, a more recent summary of these studies has confirmed this effect, although the effect size is probably much smaller than originally reported [36].

There is a suggestion that this relationship between the rate of maturation and cerebral lateralization can be found in men and women of normal genotype but homosexual orientation. As described earlier, homosexual men appear feminized in regard to measures of laterality and spatial function. They also reach puberty earlier than heterosexual men [56], and are of smaller stature [12]. The pattern of cognitive development in lesbians may be quite different from homosexual men; they show either similar or lower performance on spatial tasks than heterosexual women [59, 86], but it is not clear how this relates to their rate of maturation.

Thus, evidence for a relationship between the rate of maturation, lateralization, and cognitive function may be present in at least three groups who appear to differ in their early hormone exposure: individuals who vary by chromosomal abnormality, who differ by sex, or who differ by sexual orientation. Hence, regardless of the proximate cause, the hormonal environment appears to direct the development of cerebral lateralization. This developmental trajectory then produces subsequent changes in cognitive ability, most noticeably in the realm of spatial cognition, as would be predicted from its late development as a tertiary, right hemisphere association area.

Sexual selection and laterality

Yet such correlations between development and function simply relocate the question of cognitive sex differences to a more proximate level of analysis; they do not address the question of why males and females should mature at different rates. To answer this question, one must leave the realm of cognitive neuroscience and return to that of evolutionary biology.

The most common explanation for sexual bimaturism is that it is a mechanism by which sexual selection can act on the differential allocation to trait size. For example, dimorphism in body size is a common sexual dimorphism. It is also the direct consequence of differential growth patterns between males and females. Because growth for many vertebrate species essentially halts at puberty, individuals that mature more rapidly reach puberty at a smaller adult size. Thus, simply changing development rates produces sex differences in trait size [4].

In humans, sex differences in stature are also correlated with the age at puberty. Girls develop more quickly than boys, reaching the developmental stage where androgens halt the process of longitudinal bone growth. Most structural growth is reached by late adolescence, though approximately one to two years earlier in girls than boys, at least in westernized societies. This produces a sex difference in stature, since slower maturing individuals will be taller when they reach the stage of skeletal maturation [83].

What is the adaptive significance of such sexual bimaturism? It appears to be an adaptation for polygamy in many species [4], based on the following logic. Small males cannot compete for access to females whereas small females are not handicapped by their body size since the female's slow rate of reproduction assures that they will be the limiting sex. Hence, males will compete for females and hence males, not females, will require a larger body size to compete [19]. In highly polygynous species, where body size dimorphism is most pronounced and male reproductive success is strictly tied to body size, delayed maturation thus functions to increase competitive ability [4].

Therefore, the consequences for the rate of maturation can be subject to sexual selection. Other consequences of maturation rate, such as the differential lateralization of the brain and hence differential cognitive ability, could also be the product or side-product of sexual selection. A simple model could be constructed from the basic biology of cerebral growth vectors and sex difference in the rate of maturation that would explain sex differences in cerebral lateralization and spatial function. If this model is correct, then sex differences in cognitive function would be influenced by any factor that changes the rate of development. The faster the rate of growth or the earlier the date of puberty, the more cerebral symmetry, less right hemisphere development, and hence less specialization of spatial function. If puberty is extremely early, one would predict that left hemisphere function achieves an unnatural dominance; if puberty is extremely late, then right hemisphere function should excel.

Food, sex, and cognitive function

What factors influence the rate of development or age at puberty? One of the best studied examples is the effect of social circumstances, such as social class, westernization, or an urban lifestyle. This is clearly reflected in the patterns of body stature: over the last century, perhaps due to a twentieth-century change in diet, children have become progressively larger at all ages, resulting in an increase of about one inch per generation in added height. As a result, both men and women achieve a greater stature, and attain it in fewer years than they did a century ago. These patterns are strongly influenced, however, by social circumstances: poorer boys are significantly shorter than wealthy boys at all ages [83].

Because stature is related to age at maturity, this suggests that children are maturing at younger ages. Indeed, the age at puberty in girls has changed dramatically over the last century. Using the age at first menstruation as an unambiguous indicator of maturation in girls in six western societies, J. M. Tanner calculated that this age has dropped four years in the last century, a rate of approximately four months per decade, although the trend now appears to have stabilized at an average age of twelve to thirteen years [83].

This pattern also appears in contemporary cultures which differ in their wealth and social class, and thus perhaps in diet. Daughters of unskilled workmen in Britain reach menarche two to three months before daughters of men with managerial jobs [83]. A similar pattern is found between girls living in urban versus rural areas: the average age of puberty in girls living in Warsaw has been almost two years younger than girls living in the surrounding countryside for the past hundred years [82]. Similar patterns can be seen in comparisons of urban and rural populations in Nepal, Bolivia, and the United States [5].

These differences are probably caused by a multitude of factors, including diet, exposure to disease, stress, and even social environment [83]. For example, the rate of maturation could be a physiological response to social stress, since girls reach puberty earlier in households where the father is absent [81]. However, because diet is directly linked to the reproductive functions, such as hormone levels, ovulation frequency, etc. in humans [28], it may play an extremely important role. Under more natural conditions, such as non-industrial cultures, diet may have an even larger effect on human physiology. In a study of endocrine responses in New Guinea hunters, Carol Worthman reported that testosterone levels were twice as high in rich as in poor men [97].

A consequence of the human's sensitivity to environmental conditions is that rates of maturation may vary dramatically by culture. In New Guinea hunter–gatherer societies, puberty is not only delayed relative to industrial cultures, but is also more protracted; the typical growth spurt seen in the western adolescent is seen as a much more gradual increase in growth rate. As a result, adolescent girls and boys show more similar rates of growth; one might predict an absence of sex differences in brain organization for this reason. However, this effect is mitigated in New Guinea because of differential treatment: boys are valued more highly by parents, and therefore are fed higher quality foods, and hence this potential for developmental equality is not realized [96]. Even so, the sex difference in the age at puberty is smaller in non-industrialized societies. In this sense, the protracted adolescence, with early sexual maturity, found in western societies may be a recent artefact of our urban culture [79].

If growth acceleration exaggerates the sex difference in the age at puberty, when both males and females are developing at their maximum rate, this could theoretically produce a greater difference in cerebral laterality, with a subsequent increase in sex differences on spatial tasks. This model would reconcile two contrary observations: first, that patterns of cognitive sex differences in humans are highly conserved across cultures [34]; and second, that there are equally striking effects of social environment on the development of cognition in humans.

Research on social effects on cognitive development has concentrated on the tasks which show the largest effect size (i.e. spatial tasks showing a male advantage). Studies of spatial cognition in different societies and cultures suggest that the magnitude of sex differences are highly dependent on environmental conditions and personal history. In short, when individuals are given more freedom to explore their environment, this freedom is correlated with enhanced spatial abilities, both within and between cultures, producing either a male or female advantage, depending on the spatial ecology of the sexes in that culture (reviewed by Mary Van Leeuwen [87]). Thus, the male advantage in spatial cognition is seen in traditional Mexico City households, where girls are kept at home and boys are free to wander, whereas the identical methods, testing a ten-year sample of schoolchildren in Austin, Texas, revealed only small and insignificant differences. In Israel, the pattern of sex difference varied with Jewish subculture: among Sephardic Jews, men outperformed women, but the reverse pattern was seen in Ashkenazy communities. The female advantage seen in the Ashkenazy community might be explained by the atypical social organization of this culture. In a study of Orthodox Jews in New York City, the Sephardic pattern was seen in less traditional households: males scored higher than females on spatial tasks. The reverse was seen in more traditional households, where women obtained the higher spatial scores. The explanation offered by the author is that in strict Orthodox families, women, not men, travel outside the home to obtain goods and services and hence are more mobile than men, who are expected to remain in seclusion for serious intellectual study [87].

Such plasticity can also be distinguished within a culture: in rural Kenyan cultures, regardless of sex, children who wander farther from home, because of duties such as herding livestock, score higher on spatial tasks than children of the same age with more sedentary duties. On average, this meant that boys scored higher than girls on spatial tests, however in the few cases where girls roamed farther, they also showed superior spatial ability compared to boys of their age [65].

Thus, sex differences in spatial cognition may be enhanced or reversed by the social environment. They may also be completely eliminated. In nomadic cultures, such as the Inuit, where both men and women forage for food over large areas, there are no sex differences on any measure of spatial cognition [9].

Is there an underlying neural basis for these cultural patterns? Would, for example, greater mobility as a child lead to enhanced function in the brain structures mediating spatial learning? For example, early spatial experience could increase hippocampal development and enhance cerebral asymmetries by increasing right hemispheric growth. Although we have no data on humans, in laboratory mammals such as the rat, the hippocampus continues to add new neurons throughout life [3, 7, 50]; this is also found in other mammals (reviewed by M. S. Kaplan [49]). This rate of neurogenesis in the hippocampus appears to be related to learning, as it is linked to a physiological process underlying associative learning, long-term potentiation [98]. The hippocampus also responds to changes in the environment, even in adults. Adult rats moved to complex, semi-natural environments show structural changes in the brain after only four days, including an increase in structure in the hippocampus [45]. Finally, male rats moved to an enriched environment show changes in laterality in the hippocampus: at puberty, the dorsal hippocampus changes from a greater thickness of the right to the left side [25]. These scattered, and not always consistent, lines of evidence suggest that hippocampal plasticity, and perhaps spatial cognition, in the laboratory rat can be influenced by the social and physical environment around the time of puberty. It is perhaps not so far-fetched that in humans, too, social influences have organizational effects on brain structure, cerebral symmetry, and spatial ability.

In summary, the developmental cascade leading to the sexual differentiation of spatial cognition is determined—but only by the environment. The environment may exert its influence in different ways and at different times, beginning with the prenatal hormonal milieu, affected later by the perinatal influences of diet and other determinants of postnatal endocrinological state, and finally influenced by the culturally determined potential for exploration by the child. Thus, on the one hand, sex differences in cognitive function in humans, like those found in rodents and songbirds, may be the end-product of a long developmental cascade, canalized by the early hormonal milieu, which is in part determined by genetic mechanisms. On the other hand, if such differences are determined by such a general trait as an individual's rate of development then these differences are extremely plastic. Thus, if rate is key, then sex differences are not 'determined' at all—or only in the most minimal sense of the word.

Sexual selection and human ecology

Yet even in the midst of this complex array of environmental influences we can discern faint echoes of the sexually selected pattern seen in other species. Even the diversity of these influences cannot conceal the observation that in most cultures, when there is a sex difference in spatial cognition, it more often shows a male, not a female, advantage. What is the significance of this pattern? Again, the answer must lie in the evolutionary history of sex differences; the magnitude of a sex difference may be explained by an individual's history but the average direction of the difference can only be explained by the history of the species [38].

Just as sexual selection may produce sexual bimaturism because of the advantage of increased body size to one sex and not the other, so sexual bimaturism of the brain may also be part of a larger adaptation to greater plasticity. Environments change; the social environment changes even more quickly, since conspecifics compete with similar skills and abilities [90]. Our species is characterized by plasticity and adaptability, and perhaps this is also true for patterns of sexual dimorphisms in cognition, as is true in other species. If sexual dimorphism in height varies dramatically according to diet and culture, then perhaps cognitive sexual dimorphisms, small but persistent, reversible according to experience, are simply a subtler example of a sexually selected predilection for a male advantage on certain tasks under average circumstances.

Why would such an advantage exist in *Homo sapiens*? Cognitive sex differences in songbirds and rodents operate in the context of mate choice and mate competition, and have evolved in response to sexual selection for competitive ability. Are sex differences in human spatial abilities also subject to sexual selection? I can only join others in speculating on the possible adaptive significance of our small sex differences and their effect on the course of human evolution [80]. The scenario can be described as follows: man the hunter requires skills in throwing, aiming, and navigation in order to navigate long-distance hunting trips over large or unknown terrain, kill game with projectiles and then return home, often with a heavy meat burden, via the shortest route. Thus, hunter skills tap into the same spatial abilities assessed by laboratory tasks, which would explain the common male advantage on such tasks. Such navigational skills would be adaptive for long-range hunting, but not necessarily for short-range gathering. Here, the ability to remember the location of fruiting plants, notice and remember subtle changes in spatial distribution of food sources, and possess fine motor control for harvesting and processing fruits and seeds, would be advantageous. Thus, the female constellation of cognitive skills would adapt for gathering, which requires tracking the fine-scale spatial distribution of fruiting plants, and also have the fine motor control to manipulate and clean small food items.

One could thus interpret sex differences in cognitive skills as indications of selection for competitive ability in foraging behaviours such as hunting and gathering women, not competing for mates. This hypothesis, suggested and elaborated by Irwin Silverman and Marian Eals, seemingly reduces the need for sexual selection to act on the evolution of such sex-specific abilities, since natural selection for foraging skills would be sufficient to explain the differences [80]. Yet we can never really know to what extent evolutionary processes such as natural and sexual selection can explain sex differences in spatial ability in our species. Sexual selection could still play a role: even in this Tarzan the Hunter, Jane the Gatherer scenario, hunting prowess may affect the outcome of mate competition. In fact, good hunters are more attractive to women, even if what they hunt is not a necessary or efficient addition to the group's energetic requirements [13]. In the Ache culture of eastern Paraguay, where men must range widely in search of meat and honey, the families of good hunters do produce more surviving offspring, suggesting that women should choose mates by their hunting ability [48].

The peacock's brain

Perhaps Montaigne was right and men and women, save for culture and education, do not differ that much. Perhaps even with 85 per cent of our societies polygynous, we will never be a strongly polygynous species, and hence differences between the sexes will always be subtle. Is this the end of the story? I think there is one more insight to be gained from this discussion and that is the issue of optimization and design. Steven Gaulin and Lee Sailer once argued that among primates, the sexes were not created equal and that females could be considered the 'ecological sex'. Males 'are often larger, more flamboyant coloured, more aggressive, more mobile, more active in courtship, and more likely to bear structures such as antlers, manes, and large canine teeth that are of little or no use in exploiting nutritional resources' [35]. Thus, it is female, not male body size that is optimized for the species's ecological niche; the larger size of the polygynous male served only to increase his ability to compete with other males, and hence was adaptive but not 'ecological'.

Similarly, a Martian visiting our planet for the first time might note that one-half of the population uses their entire brain to process information, automatically integrates more incidental information, is less aggressive and more cooperative, and overall seems closer to the ideal design for a naked ape. This Martian might view traits such as superior mathematical ability or superior skill in chess as arbitrary skills that have evolved for the same reason as a peacock's tail, representing the 'investment' needed to compete successfully with other males (i.e. the typical solution of the disadvantaged sex). It is usually the male's solution: the ability to compete with other males using traits that serve no other purpose but to compete. This view of things puts a new slant on the old problem of gender and society. Suddenly, the smaller female brain is seen as a miracle of economy and design, destined to survive the turmoils of history, less likely to be disturbed during development or to suffer immune disorders [84], less likely to become involved in unnecessary and damaging acts of aggression and warfare. Thus, it is the female that is the smaller, the 'ecological' sex, best adapted to survive in the ecological niche of the species, and it is the male who carries the heavier burden or handicap [99] of sexual selection, his fitness dependent on arbitrary traits that reduce his competitive ability as a human being, although they are all too necessary for his competitive ability as a man. Thus, if brain structure and function are constrained by the ecology of the species, it may be that sex differences in cognitive traits are no more and no less important than the peacock's tail. This may not be such a bad thing for the species. It has been argued that sexual selection has served as a forge for rapid evolutionary change, proceeding more rapidly than natural selection and hence arriving more quickly at novel solutions, some of which may benefit both males and females [90]. Far from being a handicap for human evolution, it may be that we should give sexual selection some credit for the rapid evolution of our unique cognitive abilities and complex culture. For to conclude with the words of Oscar Wilde: 'Ethics, like natural selection, make existence possible. Aesthetics, like sexual selection, make life lovely and wonderful' [91].

REFERENCES

1. ALLEN, L. S. and R. A. GORSKI. 'Sexual dimorphism of the anterior commissure and massa intermedia of the human brain'. *J. Comp. Neurol.* **312**: 97–104, 1991.
2. ALLEN, L. S. and R. A. GORSKI. 'Sexual orientation and the size of the anterior commissure in the human brain'. *Proc. Natl. Acad. Sci.* **89**: 7199–202, 1992.
3. ALTMAN, J. and S. A. BAYER. 'Migration and distribution of two populations of hippocampal granule cell precursors during the perinatal and postnatal periods'. *J. Comp. Neurol.* **301**: 365–81, 1990.
4. ANDERSSON, M. *Sexual Selection*. Princeton, NJ: Princeton University Press, 1994.
5. ANGOLD, A. and C. W. WORTHMAN. 'Puberty onset of gender differences in rates of depression: A developmental, epidemiologic and neuroendocrine perspective'. *J. Affect. Disord.* **29**: 145–58, 1993.
6. ARNOLD, A. P. 'Developmental plasticity in neural circuits controlling birdsong: sexual differentiation and the neural basis of learning'. *J. Neurobiol.* **23**: 1506–28, 1992.
7. BAYER, S. A., J. W. YACKEL, and P. S. PURI. 'Neurons in the rat dentate gyrus granular layer substantially increase during juvenile and adult life'. *Science*, **216**: 890–2, 1982.
8. BEECHER, M. D., S. E. CAMPBELL, and P. K. STODDARD. 'Correlation of song learning and territory establishment

strategies in the song sparrow'. *Proc. Natl. Acad. Sci.* **91**: 1450–4, 1994.

9. BERRY, J. W. 'Temne and Eskimo perceptual skills'. *Inter. J. Psychol.* **1**: 207–29, 1966.

10. BEST, C. T. 'The emergence of cerebral asymmetries in early human development: a literature review and a neuroembryological model'. In *Brain Lateralization in Children: Developmental Implications.* Molfese and Segalowitz (eds.). New York: Guilford Press, 1998.

11. BESTON, H. *The Outermost House.* New York, NY: Viking, 1929.

12. BLANCHARD, R., R. DICKEY, and C. L. JONES. 'Comparison of height and weight in homosexual versus nonhomosexual male gender dysphorics'. *Arch. Sex. Behav.* **24**: 543–54, 1995.

13. BORGERHOFF MULDER, M. 'Human behavioural ecology'. In *Behavioural Ecology: An Evolutionary Approach.* Krebs and Davies (eds.). Oxford: Blackwell, 1991.

14. BOWERS, C. A. and R. C. LABARBA. 'Sex differences in the lateralization of spatial abilities: A spatial component analysis of extreme group scores'. *Brain and Cognition.* **8**: 165–77, 1988.

15. BREEDLOVE, S. M. 'Sexual differentiation of the human nervous system'. *Ann. Rev. Psychol.* **45**: 389–418, 1994.

16. BRENOWITZ, E. A. and A. P. ARNOLD. 'Interspecific comparisons of the size of neural song control regions and song complexity in duetting birds: evolutionary implications'. *J. Neurosci.* **6**: 2875–9, 1986.

17. CLUTTON-BROCK, T. H., F. E. GUINNESS, and S. D. ALBON. *Red Deer: Behavior and Ecology of Two Sexes.* Chicago, IL: University of Chicago Press, 1982.

18. CLUTTON-BROCK, T. H. and P. HARVEY. 'Primate ecology and social organisation'. *J. Zool. Lond.* **183**: 1–39, 1977.

19. CLUTTON-BROCK, T. H. and A. C. J. VINCENT. 'Sexual selection and the potential reproductive rates of males and females'. *Nature,* **351**: 58–60, 1991.

20. COLLAER, M. L. and M. HINES. 'Human behavioral sex differences: a role for gonadal hormones during early development?' *Psychol. Bull.* **118**: 55–107, 1995.

21. CORBALLIS, M. C. *The Lopsided Ape: Evolution of the Generative Mind.* Oxford University Press, 1991.

22. CORBALLIS, M. C. and M. J. MORGAN. 'On the biological basis

89

of human laterality: I. Evidence for a maturational left–right gradient'. *Behav. Brain Sci.* **2**: 261–336, 1978.

23. DE LACOSTE-UTAMSING, C. and R. L. HOLLOWAY. 'Sexual dimorophism in the corpus callosum'. *Science.* **216**: 1431–2, 1982.

24. DENENBERG, V. H. 'Behavioral asymmetry'. In *Cerebral Dominance: The Biological Foundations.* Geschwind and Galaburda (eds.). Cambridge, MA: Harvard University Press, 1984.

25. DIAMOND, M. C. 'Age, sex and environmental influences'. In *Cerebral Dominance: The Biological Foundations.* Geschwind and Galaburda (eds.). Cambridge, MA: Harvard University Press, 1984.

26. EALS, M. and I. SILVERMAN. 'The hunter–gatherer theory of spatial sex differences: Proximate factors mediating the female advantage in recall of object arrays'. *Ethol. Sociobiol.* **15**: 95–105, 1994.

27. EICHENBAUM, H., N. J. COHEN, T. OTTO, and C. WIBLE. 'Memory representation in the hippocampus: Functional domain and functional organization'. In *Memory: Organization and Locus of Change.* Squire, Lynch, Weinberger, and McGaugh (eds.). Oxford University Press, 1992.

28. ELLISON, P. T., C. PANTER-BRICK, S. F. LIPSON, and M. T. O'ROURKE. 'The ecological context of human ovarian function'. *Human Reprod.* **8**: 2248–58, 1993.

29. FINLAY, B. L. and R. B. DARLINGTON. 'Linked regularities in the development and evolution of mammalian brains'. *Science.* **268**: 1578–84, 1995.

30. GALEA, L. 'Sex differences in route learning'. *Univ. West. Ontario Res. Bull.* **700**: 1–40, 1991.

31. GAULIN, S. J. C. and J. S. BOSTER. 'Human marriage systems and sexual dimorphism in stature'. *Am. J. Physic. Anthropol.* **89**: 467–75, 1992.

32. GAULIN, S. J. C. and R. W. FITZGERALD. 'Sex differences in spatial ability: An evolutionary hypothesis and test'. *Am. Nat.* **127**: 74–88, 1986.

33. GAULIN, S. J. C. and R. W. FITZGERALD. 'Sexual selection for spatial-learning ability'. *Anim. Behav.* **37**: 322–31, 1989.

34. GAULIN, S. J. C. and H. A. HOFFMANN. 'Evolution and development of sex differences in spatial ability'. In *Human*

Reproductive Behaviour: A Darwinian Perspective. Betzig, Borgerhoff-Mulder, and Turke (eds.). Cambridge, UK: Cambridge University Press, 1987.

35. GAULIN, S. J. C. and L. D. SAILER. 'Are females the ecological sex?' *Am. Anthropol.* **87**: 111–19, 1985.

36. GRABER, J. A. and A. C. PETERSEN. 'Cognitive changes at adolescence: biological perspectives'. In *Brain Maturation and Cognitive Development: Comparative and Cross-Cultural Perspectives.* Gibson and Petersen (eds.). Hawthorne, NY, Aldine de Gruyter, 1991.

37. HIER, D. B. and W. F. CROWLEY JR. 'Spatial ability in androgen-deficient men'. New *Engl. J. Med.* **306**: 1202–5, 1982.

38. HINDE, R. Personal communcation, 1996.

39. HISCOCK, M., R. INCH, C. JACEK, C. HISCOCK-KALIL, and K. M. KALIL. 'Is there a sex difference in human laterality? I. An exhaustive survey of auditory laterality studies from six neuropsychology journals'. *J. Clin. Exper. Neuropsychol.* **16**: 423–35, 1994.

40. HOLMAN, S. D. and J. B. HUTCHINSON. 'Lateralized action of androgen and development of behavior and brain sex differences'. *Brain Res. Bull.* **27**: 261–5, 1991.

41. HOYENGA, K. B. and K. T. HOYENGA. *Gender-related Differences: Origins and Outcomes.* Boston, MA: Allyn & Bacon, 1993.

42. JACOBS, L. F. 'The ecology of spatial cognition: adaptive patterns of hippocampal size and space use in wild rodents'. In *Studies of the Brain in Naturalistic Settings.* Alleva, Fasolo, Lipp, and Nadel (eds.). Dordrecht: Kluwer, 1995.

43. JACOBS, L. F. 'Sexual selection and the brain'. *Trends in Ecology and Evolution.* **11**: 82–6, 1996.

44. JACOBS, L. F., S. J. C. GAULIN, D. F. SHERRY, and G. E. HOFFMAN. 'Evolution of spatial cognition: Sex-specific patterns of spatial behavior predict hippocampal size'. *Proc. Natl. Acad. Sci.* **87**: 6349–52, 1990.

45. JURASKA, J. M. 'Sex differences in "cognitive" regions of the rat brain'. *Psychoneuroendocrinology.* **16**: 105–16, 1991.

46. JURASKA, J. M. 'Sex differences in the rat cerebral cortex'. In *The Development of Sex Differences and Similarities in Behavior.* Haug, Whalen, Aron, and Olsen (eds.). Dordrecht, Kluwer, 1993.

47. JURASKA, J. M. and J. R. KOPCIK. 'Sex and environmental influences on the size and ultrastructure of the rat corpus callosum'. *Brain Res.* **450**: 1–8, 1988.

48. KAPLAN, H. and K. HILL. 'Hunting ability and reproductive success among male Ache foragers'. *Curr. Anthropol.* **26**: 223–46, 1985.

49. KAPLAN, M. S. 'Formation and turnover of neurons in young and senescent animals: an electronmicroscopic and morphometric analysis'. *Ann. NY Acad. Sci.* **457**: 173–92, 1985.

50. KAPLAN, M. S. and D. H. BELL. 'Neuronal proliferation in the 9-month-old rodent—radioautographic study of granule cells in the hippocampus'. *Exp. Brain Res.* **52**: 1–5, 1983.

51. KIMURA, D. 'Sex differences in the brain'. *Sci. Am.* **267**: 118–25, 1992.

52. Kolb, B. and I. Q. Whishaw. *Human Neuropsychology* (4th edn). New York: Freeman, 1996.

53. LINN, M. C. and A. C. PETERSEN. 'Emergence and characterization of sex differences in spatial ability: A meta-analysis'. *Child Devel.* **56**: 1479–98, 1985.

54. MACCOBY, E. E. and C. N. JACKLIN. *The Psychology of Sex Differences*. Stanford, CT: Stanford University Press, 1974.

55. MADEIRA, M. D., N. SOUSA, and M. M. PAULA-BARBOSA. 'Sexual dimorphism in the mossy fiber synapses of the rat hippocampus'. *Exp. Brain Res.* **87**: 537–45, 1991.

56. MANOSEVITZ, M. 'Early sexual behavior in adult homosexual and heterosexual males'. *J. Abnorm. Psychol.* **76**: 396–402,1970.

57. MARLER, P. and S. PETERS. 'Sparrows learn adult song and more from memory'. *Science.* **213**: 780–2, 1981.

58. McCORMICK, C. M. and S. F. WITELSON. 'Functional cerebral asymmetry and sexual orientation in men and women'. *Behav. Neurosci.* **108**: 525–31, 1994.

59. McCORMICK, C. M., S. F. WITELSON, and A. J. McCOMAS. 'Lower spatial ability in lesbians: Interaction with hand preference'. *Soc. Neurosci. Abstr.* **22**: 1861, 1996.

60. McGLONE, J. 'Sex differences in human brain asymmetry: a critical analysis'. *Behav. Brain Sci.* **3**: 215–63, 1980.

61. MITTWOCH, U. 'Changes in the direction of the lateral growth gradient in human development—left to right and right to left'. *Behav. Brain Sci.* **2**: 306–7, 1978.

62. Montaigne, M. de. *Michel de Montaigne: The essays*. Screech (ed.). London: Penguin, 1991.

63. Morgan, M. 'Embryology and inheritance of asymmetry'. In *Lateralization in the Nervous System*. Harnad, Doty, Goldstein, Jaynes, and Krauthamer (eds.). New York: Academic Press, 1997.

64. Morgan, M. J. and M. C. Corballis. 'On the biological basis of human laterality: II. The mechanisms of inheritance'. *Behav. Brain Sci.* **2**: 270–7, 1978.

65. Munroe, R. L. and R. H. Munroe. 'Effect of environmental experience on spatial ability in an East African Society'. *J. Soc. Psychol.* **83**: 15–22, 1971.

66. Murphy, D. G. M., G. Allen, J. V. Haxby, K. A. Largay, E. Daly, B. J. White *et al.* 'The effects of sex steroids, and the X chromosome, on female brain function: A study of the neuropsychology of adult Turner syndrome'. *Neuropsychologia.* **32**: 1309–23, 1994.

67. Nadel, L. 'The hippocampus and space revisited'. *Hippocampus.* **1**: 221–9, 1991.

68. Netley, C. and J. Rovet. 'Atypical hemispheric lateralization in Turner syndrome subjects'. *Cortex.* **18**: 377–84, 1982.

69. Nottebohm, F. 'Ontogeny of bird song'. *Science.* **167**: 950–6, 1970.

70. O'Kusky, J., E. Strauss, B. Kosaka, J. Wada, D. Li, M. Druhan, and J. Petrie. 'The corpus callosum is larger with right-hemisphere cerebral speech dominance'. *Ann. Neurol.* **24**: 379–83, 1988.

71. Reboreda, J. C., N. S. Clayton, and A. Kacelnik. 'Species and sex differences in hippocampus size in parasitic and non-parasitic cowbirds'. *Neuroreport.* **7**: 505–8, 1996.

72. Roof, R. L. and M. D. Havens. 'A testosterone related sexual dimorphism in the dentate gyrus of the rat'. *Soc. Neurosci.* **20**: 328, 1990.

73. Rosenberg, H. *Saul Steinberg*. New York: Knopf, 1978.

74. Sanders, G. and L. Ross-Field. 'Sexual orientation and visuo-spatial ability'. *Brain and Cognition.* **5**: 280–90, 1996.

75. Schwagmeyer, P. L. 'Competitive mate searching in thirteen-lined ground squirrels (Mammalia, Sciuridae): Potential roles of spatial memory'. *Ethology.* **98**: 265–76, 1994.

76. SEARCY, W. A. and M. ANDERSSON. 'Sexual selection and the evolution of song'. *Ann. Rev. Ecol. Syst.* **17**: 507–33, 1986.

77. SHAYWITZ, B. A., S. E. SHAYWITZ, K. R. PUGH, R. T. CONSTABLE, P. SKUDLARSKI, R. K. FULBRIGHT *et al.* 'Sex differences in the functional organization of the brain for language'. *Nature.* **373**: 607, 1995.

78. SHERRY, D. F., M. R. L. FORBES, M. KHURGEL, and G. O. IVY. 'Greater hippocampal size in females of the brood parasitic brown-headed cowbird'. *Proc. Natl. Acad. Sci.* **90**: 7839–43, 1993.

79. SHORT, R. V. 'Human reproduction in an evolutionary context'. *Ann NY Acad. Sci.* **709**: 416–25, 1994.

80. SILVERMAN, I. and M. EALS. 'Sex differences in spatial abilities: evolutionary theory and data'. In *The Adapted Mind: Evolutionary Psychology and the Generation of Culture.* Barkow, Cosmides, and Tooby (eds.). New York: Oxford University Press, 1992.

81. SURBEY, M. K. 'Family composition, stress, and the timing of human menarche'. In *Socioendocrinology of Primate Reproduction.* Ziegler and Bercovitch (eds.). New York: Wiley-Liss, 1990.

82. TANNER, J. M. 'Earlier maturation in man'. *Sci. Am.* **218**: 21–7, 1968.

83. TANNER, J. M. 'Human growth and constitution'. In *Human Biology: An Introduction to Human Evolution, Variation, Growth, and Adaptability.* Harrison, Tanner, Pilbeam, and Baker (eds.). Oxford University Press, 1988.

84. TAYLOR, D. C. and C. OUNSTED. 'The nature of gender differences explored through ontogenetic analyses of sex ratios in disease'. In *Gender Differences: Their Ontogeny and Significance.* Ounsted and Taylor (eds.). Edinburgh: Churchill Livingstone, 1972.

85. TOLMAN, E. C. 'Cognitive maps in rats and men'. *Psychol. Rev.* **55**: 189–208, 1948.

86. TUTTLE, G. E. and R. C. PILLARD. 'Sexual orientation and cognitive abilities'. *Arch. Sex. Behav.* **20**: 307–18, 1991.

87. VAN LEEUWEN, M. S. 'A cross-cultural examination of psychological differentiation in males and females'. *Inter. J. Psychol.* **13**: 87–122, 1978.

88. WABER, D. P. 'Sex differences in cognition: A function of maturation rate?' *Science.* **192**: 572–4, 1976.
89. WATSON, N. V. and D. KIMURA. 'Right-hand superiority for throwing but not for intercepting'. *Neuropsychologia.* **27**: 1399–414, 1989.
90. WEST-EBERHARD, M. J. 'Sexual selection, social competition, and speciation'. *Q. Rev. Biol.* **58**: 155–83, 1983.
91. WILDE, O. 'The Critic as Artist', in *Selected Letters of Oscar wilde*, ed. R. Hart-Davis, Oxford: Oxford University Press, 1979.
92. WILLIAMS, C. L., A. M. BARNETT, and W. H. MECK. 'Organizational effects of early gonadal secretions on sexual differentiation in spatial memory'. *Behav. Neurosci.* **104**: 84–97, 1990.
93. WILLIAMS, C. L. and W. H. MECK. 'The organizational effects of gonadal steroids on sexually dimorphic spatial ability'. *Psychoneuroendocrinology.* **16**: 155–76, 1991.
94. WIMER, R. E. and C. WIMER. 'Three sex dimorphisms in the granule cell layer of the hippocampus in house mice'. *Brain Res.* **328**: 105–9, 1985.
95. WITELSON, S. F. 'Neural sexual mosaicism: sexual differentiation of the human temporo-parietal region for functional asymmetry'. *Psychoneuroendocrinology.* **16**: 131–53, 1991.
96. WORTHMAN, C. Personal communciation, 1995.
97. WORTHMAN, C. M. and M. J. KONNER. 'Testosterone levels change with subsistence hunting effort in Kung San men'. *Psychoneuroendocrinology.* **12**: 449–58, 1987.
98. YORK, A. D., B. E. DERRICK, and J. L. MARTINEZ JR. 'Mossy fiber LTP increases neurogenesis in the adult rat dentate gyrus'. *Soc. Neurosci. Abstr.* **21**: 602, 1995.
99. ZAHAVI, A. 'Mate selection—a selection for a handicap'. *J. Theor. Biol.* **53**: 205–14, 1975.

4

A Little Learning: Women and (Intellectual) Work

MICHÈLE LE DOEUFF

When the Herbert Spencer committee honoured me with the invitation to give a lecture on women and work, I quickly realized that this is no longer a well-defined subject. It refers to a tangle of problems, and, what is more, the category of women's work itself may prove unstable, or ought to prove so. If, then, a brand new approach is necessary today, kindly consider this essay, which will broach the topic primarily from the perspective of intellectual work, as just a contribution to the necessary redefinition of the theme—a redefinition that will require many an indirect analysis. And let me tackle mine in a roundabout way.

The United Nations conference held in Cairo in 1994 made it plain that more and more agencies and governments feel concerned with the steep increase of population worldwide. Whatever the reasons for constructing the world's population as a major concern may be, this debate happens to have a side effect which will be my starting point: people in charge in the west are now realizing that 70 per cent of the children deprived of schooling are girls, and women the better part of the illiterate. How is it that a concern about population makes the issue of schooling for girls suddenly more visible? The answer is that a correlation between female illiteracy

I should like to thank Simone Oettli and Richard Scholar, who kindly checked my English and turned this task into an occasion for shared merriment.

97

and larger families, or between female literacy and smaller families, is suggested. Furthermore, this correlation is being accepted as a causality, with the result that a miracle cure is said to be in view: let us educate girls *a little* and this will work wonders.

A sample of this creed appeared in an issue of *The Economist* published in September 1994, at the time of the Cairo conference. The editors first challenged a survey carried out by demographers who had argued that 'differences in contraceptive prevalence' explained about 90 per cent of the variation in fertility rates. *The Economist* declared they could not believe this, or to quote, that they found it 'preposterous to identify contraceptive supply as the main determinant of family size'. And they claimed that 'the single most effective and enduring way of moderating population growth, even more than by the diffusion of contraception, is to give women more and better education'. As if it was either one or the other, either making contraception available or giving education to girls. As if the latter appealed to the men in charge, but not the former. The article was illustrated by a diagram, entitled 'A little learning'. Based on statistics provided by the World Resources Institute (WRI), it was supposed to show that the fertility rate drops as female literacy increases.[1]

Sometimes, statistics happen *not* to be particularly relevant or indeed reliable from a mere mathematical point of view, as in the famous quip used in epistemology classes: 'Parisians who pay a monthly rent of 8,000 francs or more tend to go skiing more frequently than people who pay a lower rent; therefore, when all the rents go up, skiing will become accessible to all'. In a similar way, with the alleged correlation between a little learning and a drop in the fertility rate, it may be simply that a higher rate of female literacy derives from a factor which also involves some drop in the fertility rate. It may well be a package: when the situation is somehow better for women, we gain access to some civil rights, to some repro-

---

[1] *The Economist*, 3 September 1994.

ductive rights, and to some schooling, along with some free speech in the household and outside it, and to some access to skilled labour outside the household, women becoming thus financially, practically, and mentally more independent. But why not ask family planning counsellors their opinion? Their experience tends to show that, when a woman has some schooling, it is indeed easier for her to choose the type of contraception she will feel happy with—the Pill or a diaphragm, or whatever—and she will handle the technique she has chosen with fewer errors. But this must be qualified straight-away: the main knowledge required is that of her own body, and some of us can still remember a time when we learned a lot about the digestive or respiratory apparatus, while the syllabus left a blank on genitalia and the reproductive process.

As a tribute to Herbert Spencer's memory, I could offer a twofold comment on this debate. *Point one*: our century believes in science, and even newspapers think it essential to offer views based on scientific or supposedly scientific data, but then they can dismiss one set of results and choose another, according to their own preference. In the example given, editors decided not to accept a demographic survey and to endorse other statistics. A major debate concerning women's lives is then offered to public opinion formulated as a learned debate, as a problem that ought to be confined in a scientific construction and left to learned experts. But the construction is based on a non-scientific element, since one set of figures was dismissed just because the editors could not believe in them—as if belief ruled science. Moreover, a critique of statistics may cast a serious doubt on the set of data produced by the WRI, with the result that we are left with the feeling that we need extremely competent feminist scientists, women who would have reached the highest level in the subject and could therefore carry out a good critical survey; namely, who could bring mathematical control to bear on the construction. It is not a *little* learning we expect from women involved in intellectual professions, but the refined capacity that makes it possible to sort out what is serious and what is not in constructions offered in the name of scientific authority.

Point two: women's liberation is not just about subtle intellectual debates, nor the critical contributions feminist scientists could make to important controversies. Women's liberation is equally about, or even more about, everyday life for every woman, whatever her social class or level of education. Now, although a basic knowledge of one's own body has been heralded as *the* crucial issue that it indeed is in every woman's life by many a feminist since at least Mary Wollstonecraft, this crucial knowledge has not been integrated to the schooling system until very recently. Some women of my generation have acquired highly sophisticated learning—in, say, Latin grammar, algebra, or Leibniz's metaphysics—while growing up with no knowledge at all about the facts of life—our life. If no knowledge of ourselves, no knowledge for ourselves was given by the education system, it did not make much difference whether we obtained a large portion of knowledge or just a small one.

Be that as it may, the philosophy behind the concept of 'a little learning for Third World women', used as a self-evident notion by (mostly male) decision-makers in the twentieth century, should give rise to some questions. Why just a little? Why not equal access to schooling? What do they call a little learning? How is the acceptable or apposite measure of learning determined? And who will determine the portion of learning which is good as opposed to the portion of learning which would be irrelevant, or possibly bad, and bad for what? When the matter discussed is what measure of learning a certain group is to be endowed with, then this limited portion of learning is always considered as a sheer means to an end, certainly not an end in itself. Moreover, it is a means not for the woman herself, but for politics, which may have little to do with her moral or practical claims. Learning, here, is seen as a mere tool in the hands of people who know its purpose and determine it.

This could be discussed in the light of Herbert Spencer's philosophy. In one of his *Essays on Education*, entitled 'What knowledge is of most worth?', he puts forth a concept which, although looking somewhat similar to 'the little learning', has in fact nothing to do with it, and obviously enough, the difference is based on gender. Spencer used the phrase 'to have some acquaintance with', stressing, for instance, that 'For the higher arts of construction, some acquaintance with the special division of Mathematics is indispensable',[2] and indeed he offers a generalization of this view, when stating that, 'to such as are occupied in the production, exchange, or distribution of commodities, acquaintance with Science in some of its departments, is of fundamental importance'.[3] This is true even for shareholders, he claims: since you buy shares in industry, and since industry is linked to technological hence scientific research, your profit or loss will depend on your understanding of the sort of sciences bearing on the business. Therefore, an acquaintance with science is vital in order to be among of the survivors in an industrial society.

In Spencer's argument, this 'acquaintance with science' was clearly related to men. The vocabulary he used made that quite obvious. No wonder, then, that he added a special section for women, and discussed what they need in order to be more competent mothers. But what did he mean, by his concept of 'acquaintance with this or that'? Not full possession perhaps, not mathematics as a mathematician would practise it, or chemistry as a chemist would, but a knowledge of elementary principles, data, and findings that would enable every man to carry out his profession and also to be a successful shareholder, since according to him, every man above the labourer is somehow a capitalist. Therefore, this is knowledge with practical aims; again, not the complete learning that scholars would have, each in their own field, but a due proportion of preparation, with social and practical activities

[2] 'What knowledge is of most worth?', first published 1859, reprinted in *Essays on Education*, London, Everyman's Library, 1911, 15.

[3] Ibid. 19.

in view. And the result of this is that one cannot discuss work without discussing education, and one must discuss education in relation to work, work as it is in a modern society.

This concept has nothing to do with 'a little learning' as defined for girls and women by a time-honoured tradition. The concept of 'some acquaintance with' means 'enough, just enough, as long as it is enough'. A due proportion, because complete knowledge is not possible. It is better to have a moderate share of more than one subject than exhaustive information bearing on just one field, and total lack of acquaintance with knowledge in other respects, Spencer claimed. Therefore the restriction is simply pragmatic: since one cannot give a boy comprehensive knowledge in all sub-jects, one must define portions that can be acquired fairly easily. Moreover, there is no gap, no difference of nature, between an elementary knowledge of, say, chemistry, for those who will be involved in this occupation and a full knowledge of chemistry for the scientist. There is a good con-tinuity between the knowledge necessary in work, whatever the occupation or job, *and* knowledge as laboured in intel-lectual professions, just as an elementary understanding is an understanding of elements of the whole.

In contrast, all we know about the western tradition con-cerning education for girls points to a difference in nature between what ought to be taught to them, and knowledge *as it is*, when it is described as full knowledge: teach her this, but, for goodness sake, do not teach her that. Teach her the tra-dition of moral thinking, both Christian and philosophical, but do not teach her history, literature, or latin. Or teach her literature, a smattering of moral philosophy and the fine arts, and of course housekeeping, but no sciences. Give her an ornamental education, but not professional training. The definition of the right syllabus for girls may vary, from one century to another, even between editions of the same book. But until recently, it was defined in such a way that it never was, nor could be, the first step leading us to intellectual work, by which I mean both the practice of an intellectual profes-

sion, as a scientist, academic, writer, researcher, *and* the practice of any profession as described by Spencer Granted, as he
claimed that most or virtually all jobs in a modern society
involve some intellectual preparation, and this applies to a
plumber, an electrician, just as much as to a lawyer, anyone
running a farm, a shop, or an artisan business, a nurse just as
much as a technical engineer, since everyone needs intellectual skills. A little learning for girls was never defined as a
portion that would be sufficient for making a living, or for
what Spencer calls self-preservation; nor was it a portion
granted provisionally, with the promise of full knowledge in
the future. A difference was always marked between 'a little
learning' for girls and free access to the learning of the
learned, but the difference also meant that women were ear-
marked for unskilled labour.

Let me bring an example of this pattern from a rightly forgotten book, which was influential thoughout Europe from
the Renaissance to the nineteenth century. Written in Latin,
it was soon translated into more than one European vernac-
ular, and I choose it because the phrase 'a little learning', '*un
petit sçavoir*', is to be found in one of the three early French
translations. The author was Vivès, a Spanish humanist based
at the English Court, as tutor to Princess Mary Tudor. His
book, the *De Institutione Feminæ Christianæ*, launched
an awkward tradition, namely the idea that a tailor-made
portion of knowledge for females is to be defined, in order to
make us more submissive to patriarchal law, more virginal
before marriage, more strictly faithful during marriage, more
compliant with any and every decision or wish of our husbands, and better mourners when widows. Vivès' plan was
based on the idea that, with a carefully selected allocation of
learning, women would be more decent, more docile, and
more chaste, than with no learning at all, because, for
instance, by giving them some kind of intellectual interest,
it would be easier to keep them at home, and they would
want to go out, dancing or socializing, less often. Also,
because learning keeps the mind occupied, whereas an idle

imagination may wander and come to mischief. But mainly because they would be given access only to books that would teach them in detail the conduct they were supposed to follow, books that would enforce duty in a deeper and more refined way. It is not necessary to give them literacy, by the way; they may listen to someone read books. And Vivès suggested a parallel between that occupation—reading or being read edifying works—and other techniques to enforce duty. Ancient Egyptians used to deprive women of shoes, so that they stayed at home; and many have thought it a good idea to deprive women of silk, pearls, and ornaments, in order to diminish their wish to go out and show off. Spinning keeps a woman at home, and when you teach a little girl her letters— if you do so, that is—she should start spinning at the same time, so that she will understand that it is one and the same thing. A little learning, therefore, is an equivalent of spinning, of being locked in, of being deprived of shoes, and I take it that Vivès recommended the use, not just of one, but of all these strategies at the same time. A little learning is viewed as a prop, among other things to enforce submission, perhaps the best of them, since it will make women internalize the demands of chastity and submission. A little learning and less freedom, in any case.

Is this idea utterly obsolete—that is, in our part of the world? Of course it is, and the younger generation would certainly laugh at the idea they could be kept at home, with no shoes, under lock and key, reading or being read edifying material, with a limited set of books and no right whatsoever to explore a library or the world of learning as they wished. Most young women would also offer some sarcastic comments on the demand for virginity. But could we, women of an already older generation, swear on oath that nothing at all of such a plan was present in our early education? I doubt we could. I suspect the demands made by schooling (learning lessons and writing essays at home in the evening, going to bed early in order to be fit the next morning) provided our parents with a formidable pretext not to allow us to go out as teenagers, and this was true even when they did not contemplate any professional outcome for our schooling or when they said we were not bright. Schooling made nice girls of us all, or was thought to help make us so, therefore it did not matter whether we found any intellectual development through it or not, and many parents thought it better we did not. Many girls of my generation were sent to school with such a double bind: learn your lessons, but learn nothing; your lessons are not devised to give you any learning, nor indeed to train you for a profession, but just to keep you in order. But this was a twofold order: we had to be nice girls, we had also to be attractive to men, and there is a long tradition of male complaints against learned women. In Spencer's words

'Men care little for erudition in women; but very much for physical beauty, good nature and sound sense. How many conquests does the bluestocking make through her extensive knowledge of history? What man ever fell in love with a woman because she understood Italian? Where is the Edwin who was brought to Angelina's feet by her German? But rosy cheeks and laughing eyes are great attractions'.[4]

Education sacrifices the body to the mind, he warned, and in a woman the body is what matters to men. We seem to be inheriting a culture which has always discussed a woman's intellectual development in relation to her sex. I say 'sex', for 'gender' would be far too polite or vague a term here. If what is at stake is rather her sex-appeal and her sexual morality, or perhaps the conflicting demands of sex-appeal and sexual morality, this must be said in so many words.

Therefore there was, or is, a huge and structural gap between intellectual work and the small ration of learning specially devised for women, a structural gap that may be noted either in theories upheld by old books or in recent practice. Some schools did their best to stick to the pattern of a specifically defined teaching for the female of the species.

---

[4] 'What knowledge is of most worth?', first published 1859, 150.

But, even in French State-run girls' schools, in which the syllabus was copied from the syllabus for boys, the underlying purpose, meaning and value of going to school could be quite different, and I believe children grasp the real reason why they go to school just as readily as they understand any portion of trigonometry, if not more readily. Similar syllabuses may well take on a completely different meaning, if the dominant view is that women should learn as little as possible or even that restrictions matter more than anything else.

According to Fénelon, a seventeenth-century writer who granted that a woman must have some education in order to govern her household, keep domestic accounts, and educate her children, there should be, in women, a sense of shame or modesty about knowledge, almost as keen as the sense of shame which inspires us with a horror of wantonness. Modesty about learning here means avoiding contact with pagan fables or other unwholesome stories and steering clear of any temptation to take a critical view on religious matters. It also means that women must not use knowledge as an adornment. And it must mean something much more than that or else Fénelon's vocabulary could not be accounted for. Furthermore, when he discusses literacy, a subtext tends to show through. A girl should be taught to read and write with correctness, she should never be at fault with her spelling; accustom her to using a neat script and making straight lines on the paper. She should be exact in her grammar, always use proper and accurate terms, neatly express her meaning, in an orderly way, etc.[5]. As if acquiring literacy were nothing more than learning tidiness, a virtue most important in women according to the author.[6] What is acquired, then, is a virtue and not a skill, the virtues of cleanliness and propriety and certainly not the beginning of intellectual accomplishment. When you come to think how dreadful the handwriting of

[5] Fénelon, *Oeuvres complètes*, Paris, 1851–52, reprinted Slatkine, Geneva, 1971, v., 593.
[6] Ibid. 592.

some male authors was, and how casual their spelling, and what a mess their manuscripts were, you may wonder whether something important is not at stake here. Descartes said about spelling that he could not care less about it, for it was the printer's job, not his, to know whether or not you should write *corps* with a p in it![7] All he was concerned about was to make the metaphysical distinction between this *corps*, the body, and the mind. Perhaps it was *infra dig* for a philosopher to know how to spell, perhaps he assumed that creative skills in the intellectual world implied a certain amount of untidiness, or at least the right not to bother too much with orderliness. Again, younger women today would simply laugh at the idea they should prove themselves tidy and law-abiding by having neat handwriting, correct spelling, and perfect grammar, but I believe this is so recent a change that many women schooled during the 1950s could bear witness that common practice was for a long time consistent with Fénelon's ideas. Even literacy, then, may function, not as a skill, but as a mere token of conformity. I believe this is the ideology at work in the World Resources Institute's views, taken up by *The Economist*: with a little learning and some literacy women create less disorder, and they internalize the order imposed upon them more readily. And since the increase of population is now being seen as a major disorder, let us conclude the syllogism and give all women a little education, which is safe anyway. It is as if a western myth were being prescribed to the rest of the world. And it is certainly a mythical medicine for overpopulation, if literacy is given instead of birth control, and not together with it. If underpopulation was found to be a disorder, perhaps they would recommend the same remedy, and claim that mothers with a little learning tend to reduce the infant mortality rate.

Another detail shows that western executives share past masters' ideology: when they refer to Third World women's access to work, they refer to cottage industries, such as sewing

[7] Descartes, 'Lettre à M . . . , mars 1638', in *Oeuvres de Descartes*, ed. by Adam and Tannery, *Correspondance*, v. II, Paris, 1898, 46.

at home. Women must be kept at home, and if they must work, let this be at home or *close to home*, as Christine Delphy and Diana Leonard entitled their book about women's work.[8] For we should all be aware that women do indeed work. According to the United Nations, women are responsible for two-thirds of the working hours on this planet. Nonetheless, the current image does not fit with those figures, for the view remains that women do not work, or only rarely, or even that there is something unnatural about a working woman, that is about a woman working outside her rightful place. Discounting most of the work done by women is achieved by a simple trick: just deem that what is done at home, or close to home, is not real work, but just something you do naturally perhaps, and certainly invisibly.

The link between home and women may explain a lot, as far as this image is concerned. It seems to be created by the demands of patriarchal fidelity. Again, virgin brides and faithful wives, fulfilling the demands of monogamy, are better kept as close to home as possible. Traditional sexual moral-ity implies an organization of space, namely, a distinction between the space in which control may be exercised, and the outer space or the world at large. This is even true when discussing access to intellectual accomplishments or skills. Consider the Platonic myth in the *Phaedrus*: eleven gods and goddesses fly to a space beyond the sky, where they feast on the contemplation of truth, justice, and wisdom; eleven deities out of twelve, because Hestia remains at home on her own. Hestia, the housewife goddess, cannot travel, and is thus deprived of access to the outerworld and to truth. The way knowledge is constructed in our culture is made plain by this Platonic myth: it has something to do with going out and circulating in the widest space possible; not being confined within a domestic space or household. I wonder if this myth is not inspiring us academics, when we long for an interna-tional lifestyle, and reject the idea of belonging just to a

---

[8] C. Delphy, *Close to Home: a materialist analysis of women's oppression*, trans. and ed. by Diana Leonard, London, Hutchinson, 1984.

limited parochial community. It can even inspire female academics, since after all, five goddesses are involved in the Platonic trip, although this may not be considered acceptable. For, in contrast, it is thought proper that women should be part of the household and should belong—in the literal meaning of the term—to a given restricted community. Therefore, the gendered distribution of space is the same, whether we discuss intellectual life or work acknowledged as such. Truth and what counts as work are to be found away from home in some outer space which is for men, or mostly for men. For decent women, what remains is a confined inner space, where no truth is, and where the only learning possible is not the real kind. And work done there is not considered real work.

The link between women and home, whether considered as natural or enforceable, could even explain how a separation between the arts and sciences took place. From the Renaissance onwards, some innovative fathers thought it possible to give their daughters not just a little learning, but a reasonably comprehensive education in the arts or humanities, since this could take place at home. On the other hand, the emergence of modern science and research was taking place outside the home, and contacts with scientific circles often implied some travelling abroad. Of course, humanities for girls gave them no future in the professions, at a time when men with such a training could become lay administrators. But for a few and brilliant exceptions, women's education in the humanities was, as Lisa Jardine has pointed out, mostly ornamental or again supposed to be a means for accomplishing virtue.[9] Modern science began as a more clearly masculine activity than the humanities, thus separating itself from the arts. This must be understood in relation to the distribution of space—science out of the home, humanities within.

[9] See Anthony Grafton and Lisa Jardine, *From the Humanism to the Humanities*, Harvard University Press, 1986, ch. 2, 'Women Humanists: Education for what?', 29ff.

If, then, the topic 'women and work, intellectual or not' must involve the consideration of 'the home', perhaps one should add that home must be understood as both a physical place (the appropriate site for a woman's work that is not work) and also a legal space, by which I mean that the fruit of her work has long been understood as belonging to the household. This was so much the case that, even when the work took place somewhere else, the wages were paid to the husband or father. In Europe, until the beginning of this century, women workers were not handed their own wages, and they often needed a husband's or a father's permission to work as servants or factory workers. The result was that even work outside the household did not help them to become more independent. It was a major breakthrough for women to be seen as the owners of their own working capac-ity—outside the home, that is.

Another step has taken place more recently, in some coun-tries at least. It does not concern housekeeping, as yet, but productive work carried out by women very close to home. A baker's wife may sell bread in the shop twelve hours a day. Nonetheless, she used to be counted as a 'married woman with no profession', which implied, *inter alia*, that none of the social protection granted to an employee, in terms of pension, health insurance, risks of redundancy, and so forth, was granted to her. Artisan's wives, women involved in agriculture, lawyers' or doctors' wives acting as secretaries, have been seen as their husbands' helpers, not as the active workers they are or as par-ticipants in a family business. It is thanks to feminist sociolo-gists that this major issue has been raised and addressed, through changes in legislation, at least in some countries. And with the increase in women magistrates and barristers, it is now possible to have such work taken into account in the divorce courts, so that a woman may get, instead of alimony, something like a retroactive salary. The court makes an esti-mate of what the work for her husband amounted to, and then she gets her due, instead of becoming somehow a 'kept' woman after the fact. This recognition of women's work as their husbands' employees is a good example of how intellectual work, carried out by women researchers, and some women's access to learned professions such as the law, may change the very concept of work, when used to describe women's work, thus improving the social status of thousands of women. From a narrow definition which counted out many working hours, we have moved to a broader one, which now includes what is done close to home.

To these practical and moral issues concerning social and legal recognition of women's work close to home, a theoretical debate is to be added. I suggested earlier that the association of women with home is a way of enforcing traditional sexual morality, with the production of a legitimate offspring at stake. That is consistent with Engels' *Origin of the Family, Private Property and the State.* But some Marxist feminists have claimed it is the other way round. According to them, exploitation of women's working potential by their husbands, or extortion of free labour, in housekeeping as well as in home-based productive work, is the core of the structure, whereas the construction of the family code and ideology is basically a technique to trap women into a position where they will work for nothing.[10] Male-centred society uses the 'bliss of motherhood' to attract women into family life, the same society deprives women of reproductive rights in order to press them into matrimony, so that they work as their husband's employees for free.

Whichever theory is right, and perhaps we should knit the two together, certainly one theoretical finding is currently accepted by all: you cannot discuss women's work without discussing in detail the sexual contract that determines the

[10] This view was held by Simone de Beauvoir in the 1970s, at a time when Feminists were fighting for the right for birth control. See her Preface to *Avortement: une loi en procès; l'affaire de Bobigny*, Paris, Gallimard, 1973, reprinted in *Les Écrits de Simone de Beauvoir*, ed. by Claude Francis and Fernande Gautier, Paris, Gallimard, 1979, 508–9. The views the text expressed may very well have been as much suggested to Beauvoir as actually held by her. For although she was never the feminist movement's spokesperson, she occasionally acted as our mouthpiece in public and we were only too glad to be her think tank.

family, or without discussing reproductive rights, at least today, when birth control can be obtained by many women. Such a theoretical principle, implying that both work and sexual contracts must be discussed together, has also been taken up by some feminist historians—let me simply quote the title of a book by Bridget Hill, *Women, Work and Sexual Politics in Eighteenth-Century England.*[11] The title itself indicates a full recognition that one cannot have 'women and work' as an independent entity or consider 'sexual politics' separately—both must be examined in relation to each other. And we would all agree that the location of women's work, namely, at home or nearby, or in the legal domain of the family, is connected with sexual reproduction and sexual relations as defined by formal or common law marriage, and sexual morality. Again, this is not gender, but sex; in this case, of course, heterosexual sex, as a relationship likely to produce children. For, when we reason in terms of gender, we tend to look for differences and to adopt only a comparative perspective. But here we must reason in terms of relationships, with the idea that the relationship between the two terms, namely, women and men, creates the social standard for both; unequal social standards of course, since one is made a dependant of the other.

And just as this situation implies an organization of space, it also involves an organization of time that must be questioned. In our culture, we believe that the daily twenty-four hours are to be divided into three parts, one for work, one for sleep, and one for leisure and all sorts of miscellaneous activities, such as trips from home to work and brushing your teeth. Such a division of time, into three parts and three parts only, has been challenged as gender-biased by Italian feminists, but let me explain the problem in my own words. This timetable could describe only a traditional man's day, the day of a man served by a wife or a mother. The only work it takes into account is productive work (as done in the office or factory)

[11] B. Hill, *Women, Work and Sexual Politics in Eighteenth-Century England*, Oxford, Blackwell, 1989.

and not what we call reproductive or regenerative work as done in the home. It is clear that from day to day the energy required to work and to live needs to be restored, obviously enough by eating. Since the clothes that a worker wears form part of his or her working potential, office workers need a clean shirt or blouse each morning, and even a mechanic's overall must be taken care of. The nation and the labour force need to keep going from one generation to the next, therefore the birth and upbringing of children is contained in the programme of what ought to be called reproductive work. Currently, most of this cooking, washing, ironing, and bringing up children falls on the shoulders of women, but this does not need to be the case forever. Therefore, a daily organization of time, from the point of view of women, or men with no female helper, and ultimately of couples who live according to the principle of sex equality, ought to be a partition not into three but into four parts—one for sleep, the length of which is not negotiable, one for leisure, one for productive work, and one for reproductive work.

Otherwise, time and energy for this yet unacknowledged work are stolen from women's leisure, sleep, and capacity to be involved in independent productive work. Making reproductive working hours visible and acknowledged means no longer calling housework by that name, insisting that some tasks could be carried out outside home (think of crèches and nursery schools within this framework), and discussing how we are to reduce the standard length of productive work, so that everyone can do their due share of reproductive work and have an independent productive work position. It would also alter the structure of further education. Further education is a way of renewing or increasing a person's working potential; it is an opportunity to have this potential restored. It is often denied to women, especially women with young children. On the other hand, when granted to a man, it often takes place at the expense of his wife, since he would cease to carry out the small fraction of reproductive work he used to do. It is not just the employer or the state that pays for it, then; it is also the female partner who is, again, working in order to help a man maintain his work potential.

This concept of reproductive work may prove revolutionary in the future. It could put an end to the endless debate for and against payment for housework. It could also settle a question concerning values. Because, after all, do we human beings love work so much, and do we believe it is the only road to salvation, as Max Weber would put it? Are women identifying with men's values when we assume that access to the labour market is an important aspect of our liberation process? Problems like this should not be discussed in these terms, but rather described on the basis of a full recognition of how things stand. Productive and reproductive work do exist, and there is a limit to the quantity of working hours a human being can stand, day after day and year after year.

To conclude, I should like to leave the floor to Immanuel Kant and to some women in developing countries. Kant claimed that professional people with a university education, clergymen, lawyers, and doctors, were instruments of government, their function being to enforce regulations concerning spiritual, social, or bodily well-being, as defined by the State. From such a perspective, it was clearly unsafe to allow women into higher education, since some of us have, after all, questioned the conceptual framework of the rules, instead of duly putting them into operation, and since we still work to redefine them for the benefit of all women. Also, please note that I have not mentioned the research carried out in social and legal studies about sexual harassment in the workplace. There is a lot to be said about the broadest learning of women who know what solidarity with others means, a lot about their real commitment to intellectual work. But there is also a lot to be said about the smallest portion of learning, as long as it is not provided to make us 'nicer'.

Some years ago, at Queen Elizabeth House Oxford, UK, I heard a lecture on teaching literacy to African adult women. The speaker mentioned that, at the end of a course, she asked her trainees what benefits they thought literacy was giving them, and the answers included the ability to read the printed instructions on medicine boxes and sorting out administrative paperwork. What is at stake here is no less than taking care of the body and dealing with the State or civil society. I remembered fondly my two grandmothers, who belonged to the first generation of girls sent to primary school in Brittany, and who were delighted at acquiring literacy. It boosted their self-esteem, was useful for many practical matters, and for reading newspapers, and, above all, it was fun, just as doing philosophy is pleasurable for me. We do not need to see a gap between a little learning and intellectual professions for women, if—but only if—the portion secured, whatever it is, opens a door to a larger and more vivid world.

5

Victims No Longer: Feminism and the Reform of Criminal Law

GERMAINE GREER

The title of this essay invokes the newest and most controversial aspect of modern criminology, namely theories of victimization. The study of the role of the victim in the precipitation of crime began with Wolfgang's work on homicide in 1958[1] and reached its nadir in 1971 in an article entitled 'Victim-precipitated Forcible Rape' by Wolfgang's student Menachem Amir, in which he argued that 20 per cent of rape victims had some record of prior sexual misconduct, such as prostitution or juvenile intercourse, and another 20 per cent had 'bad reputations'.[2] Feminists responded angrily to Amir's inept and unscientific analysis but, on the principle that what goes around comes around, Amir's work is in process of revaluation.

Actually, Amir was either too far ahead, or too far behind, his times. The 1970s were politically charged in criminology as well as in society at large with much concern about victim blaming and women's rights. Research on rape would shortly be correctly done only by women. The idea that men had anything reasonably objective to say about rape was not given much credence. Surely this overstates the matter, but there is no mistaking the fact that there are very few male authors on rape and Amir himself took an

[1] M. E. Wolfgang, *Patterns in Criminal Homicide* (Philadelphia: University of Pennsylvania Press, 1958).
[2] Menachem Amir, *Patterns in Forcible Rape* (University of Chicago Press, 1971).

117

academic assignment in Israel never really to publish in rape again. The concept of victim precipitation remained comatose under the feminist assault never to resurface, even for homicide.[3]

The tone of the article reveals the sex of the authors, who are in fact Robert F. Meier, professor and chair of sociology at Iowa State University, and Terance D. Miethe, an associate professor of criminal justice at the University of Nevada. They are wrong about studies of rape being acceptable solely from the hands of women; the hundreds of sociobiological accounts of the importance of rape amongst sticklebacks and the prevalence of sexual harassment among brown-breasted boobies that are published every year are written by men.[4]

It is certainly true that feminists reject the tendency of

---

[3] R. F. Meier and T. D. Miethe, 'Theories of Victimisation', *Crime and Justice: A Review of Research*, **17** (1993), 463; E. A. Fattah, 'Victims and victimology: the facts and the rhetoric', *International Review of Victimology*, **1** (1989).

[4] E.g. 'Heterosexual raping in the mole crab', *Emerita Asiatica, International Journal of Invertebrate Reproduction*, **1** (1979); R. Thornhill, 'Rape in *Panorpa* scorpionflies and a general rape hypothesis', *Animal Behaviour*, **28** (1980); W. H. Cade, 'Alternative male strategies: genetic differences in crickets', *Science*, **212** (1981); A. Codric-Brown, 'Reproductive success and the evolution of breeding territories in pupfish (*Cyprinodon*)', *Evolution*, **31** (1977); J. A. Farr, 'The effects of sexual experience and female receptivity on courtship rape decisions in male guppies, *Poecilia reticulata*, Pisces: *Poeciliidae*', *Animal Behavior*, **28** (1980); S. T. Emlen and P. H. Wrege, 'Forced copulations and intra-specific parasitism: two costs of social living in the white-fronted bee-eater', *Ethology*, **71** (1986); G. Jones, 'Sexual chases in sand martins (*Riparia reparia*): cues for males to increase their reproductive success', *Behavioral Ecology and Sociobiology*, **19** (1986); A. D. Afton, 'Forced copulation as a reproductive strategy of male lesser scaup: a field test of some predictions', *Behavior*, **92** (1985); F. McKinney, S. R. Derrickson, and P. Mineau, 'Forced copulation in waterfowl', *Behavior*, **86** (1983); K. M. Cheng, J. T. Burns, and F. McKinney, 'Forced copulation in captive mallards (*Anas platyhynchos*): II. Temporal factors', *Animal Behavior*, **30** (1982); P. Mineau and P. Cooke, 'Rape in the lesser snow goose (*Anser caerulescenscaerulenscens*)', *Behavior*, **20** (1979); B. Ghosh, D. K. Chouduri, and B. Palk, 'Some aspects of the sexual behaviour of stray dogs', *Applied Animal Behavior Science*, **13** (1984); J. T. Hogg, 'Mating in bighorn sheep: multiple creative male strategies', *Science*, **225** (1985); R. D. Nadler, 'Sexual aggression in the great apes', *Annals of the New York Academy of Science*, **528** (1988), and so forth. This line of argument was reviewed by L. Baron, 'Does rape contribute to reproductive success? Evaluation of sociobiological views of rape', *International Journal of Women's Studies*, **8** (1985).

victim studies to emphasize the role played by the victim in the genesis of an offence, but 'victimization' in another sense is an important part of the feminist critique of crimes against women. Far more important than Amir's unscientific ponderings about rape victims in developing modern theories of victimization have been the investigations of actual prevalence of crime as distinct from the statistics of reported crime. Although criminology is still mostly concerned with the relatively small proportion of offenders that is successfully prosecuted, attempts are being made to assess the extent of criminal behaviour as experienced by the general population by administering questionnaires to a sample population. The trail was blazed by the US President's Commission on Law Enforcement and the Administration of Justice which reported as long ago as 1967 that in a sample of 10,000 households the incidence of rape was three and a half times the reported rate. This provided the model for a number of different series of systematic investigations. The British Crime Survey is based upon the model of the US National Crime Survey that since 1972 has annually reported on a sample of 60,000 households.[5] Retrospective analysis of the data provided by such surveys has revealed problems, such as that offences that were in fact reported were not admitted in replies. Although the data should probably be regarded as relatively soft it is apparently again a case of under-reporting rather than the opposite. A similar kind of investigation was carried out by the London Rape Crisis Centre, now deprived of its funding, in order to establish the average woman's experience of rape and sexual assualt. From such studies emerge findings such as that in the United States, 38 per cent of women experience sexual molestation in youth, 24 per cent endure rape in marriage, and nearly half are victims of

[5] P. H. Ennis, *Criminal Victimization in the United States: A Report of a National Survey, National Opinion Research Centre, University of Chicago* (Washington, DC: US Government Printing Office, 1967). See also J. Garofalo and M. J. Hindelang, *An Introduction to the National Crime Survey* (Washington, DC, Law Enforcement Assistance Administration, National Criminal Justice Information and Statistics Service, 1977).

rape or attempted rape at least once in a lifetime, some repeatedly, some at the hands of groups of men, nearly all at the hands of men they know; 85 per cent of women working outside the home will be at some stage sexually harassed by an employer.

Such behaviours are apparently to be expected; men must 'have a go' and women must resent and remember it.[6] The law adopts the viewpoint of the men who must 'have a go' and is reluctant to criminalize their light-hearted predations. The law does not espouse the notion of outrage that fuels feminist encouragement of women to put an unsporting construction upon male friskiness and call sexual byplay and horsing around by its proper name, sexual molestation. Recognizing that sexual harassment of women by men is endemic is unlikely to lead to ostracism of the perpetrators. Criminal behaviour being by definition abnormal, at the same time that feminists demonstrated that molestation is part of the everyday interchange between males and females, they also demonstrated the impossibility of using the existing criminal law to find redress. What ensued was a period of confusion in which complaints proliferated, more prosecutions were brought, and fewer than ever were successful. In order to obtain redress a molested woman has to maximize the offence and to assert the male's power to disconcert, terrify, and even to destroy her. She has to prove beyond doubt that she is a genuine victim, by displaying psychic wounds that also have the potential for disqualifiying her as a witness. It is one of the bitterest ironies of rape prosecution that the women who suffer the worst psychological sequelae may be considered useless as witnesses for the crown because they may be unable to remain coherent under cross-examination.

[6] See, e.g., L. A. Curtis, *Violence, Race and Culture* (Lexington, MA: Lexington, 1975); S. F. Messner, 'Regional and racial effects on the urban homicide rate: the subculture of violence revisited', *American Journal of Sociology*, **88** (1983); L. Baron and M. A. Straus, 'Cultural and economic sources of homicide in the United States, *Sociological Quarterly*, **29** (1988).

When a woman wishes to chastize her molester and to cause him to desist in his unwelcome attentions, she has no option but to appeal to a patriarchal institution, to present herself as a victim and to exaggerate her own helplessness, because she is in a filial situation. Her passivity and helplessness are insisted upon; if she were to punch the offender in the eye, she would be guilty of assault. She would also have placed herself in the position of the kind of victim who initiates a violent interchange ands then gets the worst of it, becoming the commonest kind of victim perpetrator.

In 1948, Von Hentig listed as typical victims: 'the young, the female, the old, the mentally defective, the depressed, the acquisitive, the lonesome, the heartbroken'.[7] He should have included 'the poor'. It is certainly true that youth is a factor in victimization; the most likely victim of a homicide in Britain in 1993 was a child not yet one year old. But how important is gender as a factor in victimization? A glance at world statistics raises more questions that it answers. In the developed world, 4.4 per cent of females die of injuries, of one sort or another, compared with 10.3 per cent of males. In Latin America and the Caribbean, life is significantly more dangerous for males, 13.9 per cent dying of injuries, while the figure for females rises only to 4.8 per cent. The most dangerous country for females is understood to be China, with 10 per cent of females dying of injuries compared with 12.2 per cent of men. The safest area for men might appear to be India, where only 7.3 per cent of males will die as a result of injury, whereas 5.7 per cent of women will meet that fate. Higher mortality from injury for males is usually construed as a result of automobile and industrial accident; the Chinese figure contains an estimate of the extent of female infanticide, the Indian of dowry deaths.[8]

---

[7] H. Von Hentig, *The Criminal and his Victim: Studies in the Sociobiology of Crime* (New Haven: Yale University Press, 1948).

[8] C. J. L. Murray and A. D. Lopez, 'Global and regional cause-of-death patterns in 1990', *WHO Bulletin*, **72**: 3 (1994); M. Natarajan, *Victimization of Women: A Theoretical perspective on Dowry Deaths in India*.

Even from the cloudy vastnesses of these figures one thing emerges with clarity, that males are always and everywhere more likely to die a violent death than females. In the culture of violence the rule is 'kill or be killed' actually means 'kill *and* be killed'; of the 606 culpable homicides recorded in Britain for 1993, 375 of the victims were male and 231 female.[9] These figures compare with American FBI statistics of 60 per cent of homicides as male on male, compared with 24 per cent as male on female.[10] Of the 70,000 or so people maliciously wounded in Britain each year about two-thirds will be young males. Likewise, the most likely perpetrators are young males, although in 1993, 59 British women did murder and 6,449 did wound. Our sons are always and everywhere in more danger than our daughters, both of committing crimes of violence and being the victims of crimes of violence, but it is our daughters we are afraid for and whom we teach to be afraid for themselves. When questioned about the fear of crime young men confess to feeling least; the indices of women's fear of crime are three times those of men.[11] That fear has been taught women by those who want to protect them. We tell our daughters not to speak to strange men, not to dawdle when they are running errands, to come straight home from school. In 1990, during an umpteenth rape scare police visited university campuses to warn young women and to advise them to attend self-defence classes.[12] As a fellow of a Cambridge women's college, I cannot fail to be aware of students' perennial concerns about security; every year we are asked to install even more security lights, to eliminate shadows, to cut down shrubberies, to organize cross-campus buses, so that our students may feel less vulnerable.

[9] *Criminal Statistics for England and Wales 1993* (London, Her Majesty's Stationery Office Statistical Service).

[10] Nanci Koser Wilson, 'Gendered interaction in criminal homicide', *Homicide: The Victim/Offender Connection*, ed. A. Victoria Wilson (Cincinnati, OH: Anderson, 1993).

[11] Elizabeth Anne Stanko, 'Ordinary fear: women, violence and personal safety', in *Violence against Women: The Bloody Footprints*, ed. Pauline B. Bart and Eileen Geil Moran (Newbury Park, CA: Saga, 1993), 154.

[12] Stanko, 156.

The result seems to be that they feel even less safe; the occasional attacks on women students still occur. Meanwhile, our college grounds and corridors and rooms are full of men who are free to come and go as they please at all hours of the day and night.

Homicide figures for England and Wales tell us that 40 per cent of the women who suffered a violent death at the hands of a man were killed by their spouse or lover, 22 per cent by a family member, and 19 per cent by someone who was known to them. Only 12 per cent were known to have been killed by a stranger, and yet it is strangers that women are taught to be afraid of.[13] If anyone should be afraid of strangers it is men, for the largest proportion of men killed, 38 per cent, were killed by strangers, only 35 per cent by people known to them, 12 per cent by family members, and 6 per cent by a spouse or lover. Yet we do not tell men to avoid places of promiscuous resort or of known danger. Victimology studies tell us that there are such things as dangerous places and that the people who resort to them are taking a risk. Dangerous places are 'where the action is'.

Feminists have argued that the emphasis upon women as victims, as subjects of attack, functions as an instrument of social control.[14] The effectiveness of this kind of brainwashing was brought home to me recently. When I was walking my dogs on an old Roman road, I saw a man standing fifty yards or so ahead half-hidden in the bushes. I had to force myself to keep walking. I could only hope that my dogs, who have been taught to love everybody, would make an exception for the man who had immediately stepped back in the bushes out of sight. For as long as I walked the path I was in

[13] On 4 January 1996, the *Independent* newspaper reported a survey conducted by a motor leasing and retailing group that had found that nearly three in five women feared being attacked in their cars. One in four said she was not prepared to drive alone at night on motorways or country roads; 60 per cent felt even more vulnerable on public transport.

[14] S. Riger and M. T. Gordon, 'The fear of rape: a study in social control', *Journal of Social Issues*, **37** (1981); M. Warr, 'The fear of rape among urban women', *Social Problems*, **32** (1985); M. T. Gordon and S. Riger, *The Female Fear* (New York: Free Press, 1989).

that unknown man's power. The more dangerous he was, the more likely he was to have known that his inexplicable appearance and disappearance were menacing. The breather on the telephone, the obscene caller, the man who follows a woman in the street or chases her car on the motorway, the man who displays his penis, all such men are sniffing for the scent of female fear. Submissive behaviour on the part of the female is their reward.

Some feminists have tried to counter this kind of victimization by teaching women self-defence, principally as a cure for fear. Self-defence is fine as long as you are not physically weaker or less agile than your assailant. Most of the men who are killed by other men have been involved in a violent interchange in which defence and aggression have become confused. To be ready to defend oneself is certainly better than cringing beneath any and every kind of assault, but should a woman carry a cosh on her key chain or keep mace in the glove box of her car? Should she attempt to mimic the alien culture of violence? The men who live within the culture of violence are there because they enjoy it; they become hooked on the adrenaline rush of living dangerously. Is a woman who trains seriously in order to feel less vulnerable likely to get the same fierce pleasure out of displaying her power over weaker or more cowardly people? To spend time toughening oneself up and learning how to hurt other people is to rob other more congenial activities of that time. The woman who prepares for combat is, from one point of view at least, seriously victimized, because she has had to capitulate to an ever-present vision of herself as the object of attack. The only sure inference we can make about the woman who carries a cosh on her key-chain, after all, is that she is frightened.

Perhaps men, like dogs, unconsciously scent fear, find it gratifying and exciting and ultimately interpret it as a cue for attack. Men who are afraid of other men reassert themselves by making women afraid of them. One aspect of victimization that has been very little investigated is the extent to which seeing oneself as a victim prompts victim-type behaviour and whether victim-type behaviour inspires the offence against the person. A person who begs 'Please don't hurt me' may be introducing the idea of attack into a so far uncommitted interchange. We are told that screaming is a good idea, but is it? What is a wimp after all, but a frightened person? In the animal kingdom fear and flight inspire pursuit and kill. The scent of fear is a stimulus to all carnivores including man. Children will gang up on a frightened child and punish that child for expressing fear. By inculcating fear and encouraging fearfulness we may place women and children in jeopardy, but there seems no other option. If we are encouraging women and children to behave as quarry are we not pandering to the male's fantasy of himself as predator?

The alternative, to encourage bravado, might be to reap the whirlwind that catches up most of the men who die at the hands of other men. Men's experience of violence seems to show that refusing to feel fear is more dangerous than showing it. The infants who are murdered every year are incapable of feeling fear; they do not understand that keeping on crying will place them in extreme jeopardy and so they die. Time and again we read of little girls who were beaten to death because they would not shed tears or beg for mercy, 'naughty', 'sulky', 'rebellious', that is to say, proud and brave little girls.

Female fearfulness may be, like the timorousness of rabbits or deer, adaptive. To suppose this is to suppose that males actually are predators and females their prey, a situation which, if it exists, needs to be neutralized by civilization, rather than enshrined in statute and in custom.[15] The truth seems to be that female fearfulness is a cultural construct, instituted and maintained by both men and women in the interests of the dominant, male group. The myth of female

---

[15] Sex as predation is explicit in what baseball players used to call 'shooting beaver' that is, going to great lengths to spy out a woman undressing and gathering to watch her from the best vantage point. Gang rape is the logical extension of gang voyeurism, and has a similar connection with male bonding in sport, P. Reeves Sanday, *Fraternity Gang Rape: Sex, Brotherhood and Privilege on Campus* (New York University Press, 1990).

victimhood is emphasized in order to keep women under control, planning their activities, remaining in view, telling where they are going, how they are getting there, when they will be home. The father who insists on picking his teenage daughter up if she is out at night and bringing her home in his car is unconsciously instilling fear into her at the same time that he consciously exercises control over her. His teenage son is at more risk, but the gendered nature of fearfulness means that his father may not insist on and is unlikely even to contemplate driving him home. The myth of female victimhood keeps women 'off the streets' and in the place of most danger, at home.

The atmosphere of threat that women feel surrounded by is mostly fraudulent. The sight of a man exposing his genitals, significantly referred to as 'himself', causes fear; the man who exposes 'himself' is almost always rewarded by the sight of submissive behaviour as women passing by avert their eyes and hasten their steps. Submissive behaviour may be what he can exact by no other means. In the case of flashing, the proper response would seem to be hilarity and ridicule, to deny the flasher his kick. To complain to police is to reinforce the flasher's belief in the power of his penis to amaze and appal. In truth, the man standing with his pants down is extremely vulnerable, not least through the thin-skinned genitalia themselves. In a society where women had not been successfully victimized a man who displayed his genitalia to passing women and girls would inspire ridicule rather than dismay. He could expect to be stripped of his trousers and driven through the town, stood in the pillory maybe, naked from the waist down for a day or two, and pelted with kitchen refuse. What women feel in the late twentieth century has been investigated by Sandra McNeill who lists three stages of reaction, first, fear, shock, and disgust, then anger or outrage, then guilt, shame, or humiliation.[16] When she asked

[16] Sandra McNeill, 'Flashing: its effect on women', *Women, Violence and Social Control*, ed. Jalna Hanmer and Mary Maynard (Basingstoke: MacMillan, 1987) 100.

the women what they were afraid of, she expected them to say 'of rape'. What they said was that they were afraid of death.[17] Why should a woman who sees a man with his pants open with 'turkey-neck and gizzard' hanging out feel mortal fear? A middle-aged woman used to enjoy trotting around Cambridgeshire villages naked under an army greatcoat. 'What do you think of that then', she would say to surprised shoppers, as she held the coat open. 'Very nice, dear', they would say. Women are deemed incapable of indecent exposure. A woman's body signifies nothing; a man's body, or rather the attachment to a man's body, signifies power over life and death.

Indecent exposure began its existence as an offence under the criminal law in 1824 as a section of the vagrancy act; and applied to any man caught 'wilfully openly lewdly and obscenely exposing his person with intent to insult any female'. The wording had to be specific because penises were relatively often seen when men urinated; presumably ladies who had penises flapped at them in the 1820s were annoyed rather than frightened and complained of an impertinence rather than a threat. The connection seems to have been made with excretion rather than with rape or death. In the hundred and seventy years intervening the symbolic importance of the phallos has grown as its visibility has waned. At the close of the twentieth century the penis is the one part of the human body that has not been explored in all its variety and detail; instead it is hinted at in the advertising imagery of chocolate bars that explode in the mouth, in the silhouettes of weapons of mass destruction, and the shapes of vehicles that cleave the universe. With the disappearance of the actual penis from common view and its replacement by the fantasy phallos has come the thoroughly modern anxiety about penis size, which coupling is just what a social anthropologist would expect.

[17] Ibid. 102.

The women in McNeill's sample interpreted the act of unveiling the penis in this way:

He was saying 'I might be an old slob but I've still got more power than you have. I've still got this. I can keep you under control.'[18]

And what did she say? In all likelihood she said nothing. She wanted to say 'You can't do this to me'. By saying nothing she said 'You can do this to me'. Another woman wondered, 'Why should I feel embarrassed? I was totally humiliated'.

In fact, the old slob had no power over the woman that the woman herself did not grant him; if she threw a stone hard at his crotch, he would soon discover the real vulnerability of his genitalia. Reporting indecent exposure to the police is mostly useless because the offence must be witnessed by the arresting officer at the time of the arrest. More important, in my feminist scheme of things, is the consideration that to complain to the police, rather than throwing a pail of slops over the reprobate, is to be obliged to exaggerate the power of the male pudenda by claiming lasting disruption of the equilibrium of the complainant at the mere sight of them. The complainant is obliged to lose her time and trouble and tangle up a lot of public money in attempting to discipline a nuisance.

In 1993, Jalna Hanmer and Sheila Saunders said of a series of sexual offences against women, the touching up by a seventy-year-old man of an eighteen-year-old woman as she got on to a bus, flashing, an old man masturbating in front of a visitor, 'These crimes may legally be minor, while the impact on women may be major'.[19] It is my opinion, considered and reconsidered over forty years, that the only way forward

---

[18] McNeill, 104. See also Sheila Jeffreys, 'Indecent exposure', *Women against Violence against Women*, ed. D. Rhodes and Sandra McNeill (London: Obly Women Press, 1985).

[19] Jalna Hanmer and Sheila Saunders, *Women, Violence and Crime Prevention: A West Yorkshire Study* (Aldershot: Avebury, 1993) 344–5.

is to work to reduce the impact of such misdemeanours on women, rather than to expect the courts to track down all offenders and invoke the law in all its severity. It is up to women to render the exposure of the male organ as trivial and meaningless as the intentionally grotesque exposure of women's bodies already is. The penis is not, and should not be treated as, an awesome thing. By protesting against the exposure of male genitalia as a crime against the body politic we exaggerate the disruptive power of the phallos. The most pressing need must be to demystify the penis; to perpetuate the mystique of the penis, even the flaccid penis, as a weapon is to act in our own worst interest. Of all the parts of a man that can hurt, a penis can hurt the least. The penis is not the problem.

Amongst the more Laputan of sexologists' activities are the series of attempts carried out since the 1960s to identify potential sex offenders by measuring changes in the volume and turgidity of the penis in response to visual stimuli; the criteria are so garbled, the data derived so contradictory and unreliable, that a dispassionate observer is prompted to wonder why these investigations continue.[20] Why are researchers committed to the idea of actual visual stimuli as crucial, and to penile response as evidence of paraphilia? You would think that the penis was a self-regulating predator responding to the owner's eyes as if they were in its own head. One sex researcher struggled to account for his colleagues' fixation on the penis as signifier in this way

... from ancient times Christian theologians also regarded the penis as evil and a shameful reminder of our animal natures. The fact that we call them private parts, which must never be exposed in public, adds to our fear and anxiety. The fear persists because, just as men in the Western world believe that the head is the seat of the soul, they are equally deluded in thinking that sexuality exists in the

---

[20] Dennis Howitt, *Paedophiles and sexual offences against children* (Chichester: Wiley, 1995). See, for example, C. M. Earls and J. Proubo, 'The differentiation of francophone rapists and nonrapists using penile circumferential measures', *Criminal Justice and Behavior*, **13** (1986).

penis. This may explain our longstanding anxiety about its size and the current zeal to find causes of sexual aggression in the frequently measured but highly overrated appendage.[21]

It is evident from the word 'our' that the writer of this and the anxiety are both male. My own reading of the case would be that the penis must never be exposed in public *in order* to instil fear and anxiety; the appearance of the unveiled phallos is meant to cause shock and abasement, like the glimpse of the face of the Mikado. The penis is too sacred and too powerful to be exposed to the common gaze. Every time the flasher exposes what we dub 'himself', he receives verification from the startled and evasive behaviour of others that he is the proprietor of a sacred and powerful totem. Pornography not only reifies the female but glorifies the penis, by refusing to show it in pictures and presenting it in the text as something as large, hard, and packed with energy as an unexploded bomb. The use of the vocabulary of weaponry, to describe ejaculation, actually a fairly gentle business, as shooting and exploding, adds to the fantasy empowerment of the penis, purveyor of bliss and destruction. Anxiety about penis size may well be encoded anxiety about the perceived difference between the actual behaviour of the average unreliable and unemphatic penis and the penis of fantasy. Overestimation of the extent to which a rogue penis can damage a woman by simply being inserted into her vagina is essential to such masculinist fantasy. The incapable penis is least capable of damaging the vagina that is constructed specifically to accommodate it. Here is a description by Donna B. Schramm of the horror of rape

Rape can be the most terrifying event in a woman's life. The sexual act or acts performed are often intended to humiliate and degrade her: bottles, gun barrels or sticks may be thrust into her vagina or anus; she may be compelled to swallow urine or perform fellatio

---

[21] C. Greenland, 'The treatment and maltreatment of sexual offenders: ethical issues', in *Human Sexual Aggression: Current Perspectives*, ed. R. A. Prentky and V. L. Quinsey (Annals of the New York Academy of Science, 528, New York Academy of Science, 1988) 377–8.

with such force that she thinks she may strangle or suffocate; her breasts may be bitten or burned with cigarettes.[22]

Most of these acts could be performed by someone without a penis. By choosing to describe the horror of rape in terms of generalized sexual assault Schramm raises the possibility that the least terrifying kind of sexual assault is the actual rape. Moreover, the fact that a sex act may be meant to humiliate and degrade should not necessarily mean that it does humiliate and degrade. We do not have to accept the rapist's script. An essential aspect of women's being victims no longer is their rejection of the script that portrays the penis as a devastating weapon. The extent to which women have adopted and adapted that script was memorably illustrated when Lorena Bobbitt cut off her husband's penis instead of his head. It is illustrated every time women against rape suggest that castration would be an appropriate punishment.

It should be our intention actually to deny the rapist's script. That we do not is because more than being afraid of being raped we are afraid of being killed. Margaret Atwood once asked a group of men why they found women threatening. 'We are afraid that women will laugh at us' they said. And she asked a group of women why they felt threatened by men, 'We're afraid of being killed', they said. The men's acknowledgment to Atwood can be translated to mean that they would not tolerate verbal insurrection, abuse, ridicule, or nagging. To refuse to kowtow the holy phallos, to make light of a man's equipment is understood to be an offence against the sacred core of masculinity. In all the cases involving a female victim where a murder charge is commuted to one of manslaughter the defence is provocation, aka nagging. Judges are deeply moved by the murderer's descriptions of the intense mental anguish caused by women's words, much less moved than they are of the descriptions of the continued battery and bestial abuse of a wife who, like Ulysses,

---

[22] Donna B. Schramm, 'Rape', in *The Victimisation of Women*, ed. Jane Roberts Chapman and Margret Gates (Beverly Hills CA: Sage, 1978), 53.

waits until the ogre is asleep before she dares to try to take his life.

In the post-feminist backlash it is sometimes claimed that because of women's liberation women are becoming as lawless and violent as men. In fact, nothing has happened to alter the balance of power between men and women in this regard. Despite the lesser tolerance of violence in women on the part of the courts and the greater willingness of judges to order custodial sentences for women, the disproportion between the numbers of males and females indicted for crimes of violence is still overwhelming; women are accused of about 10 per cent of violent crime and the percentage falls much lower if we consider women under the age of eighteen, who hardly figure in the figures for assault, despite contemporary fantasies of gangs of black girls terrorizing the run-down inner city. Indeed, the proponents of self-defence training for women should bear in mind that violence exercised by women is considered more aberrant than male violence which is considered part of normal male behaviour, and the treatment of violent women by the courts is much harsher than the treatment of violent men. There is still an embedded cultural expectation that women are non-violent and have no right to expression of feeling in physical violence, with its concomitant that men under the stress of strong feeling will pound something. Although women may be thought to have a compensatory right to verbal violence or nagging, it is accompanied by an understanding that physical violence on the part of the male is an appropriate response to verbal violence on the part of the female. Men who have successfully alleged continual verbal onslaught on the part of the women they murdered continue to walk free from the courts. The woman who ridicules her husband's sexual performance, belittling the sacred phallos, as it were, is asking for it. Those of us who are aware that women unpack their hearts with words precisely because they can take no form of effective action to change their intolerable situations must see these decisions as compounding the oppression of women. In these women anger has overcome fear, and yet they are still seen as appropriate victims. Reviews of cross-cultural studies of spouse abuse all come to the same conclusion

Domestic violence is not caused primarily by mental illness, alcoholism, pathological marriage relationship, status imbalance, or stress. Family violence is best understood from a cultural perspective.[23]

What they find is that the more rigidly a culture prescribes and enforces gender roles the more likely are women to be abused by spouses.[24] Currently, a significant cluster of crimes is defined by the gender of the victim, a circumstance which implies that the sexes are actually anything but equal before the law. Sexual assaults upon males are distinguished from sexual assaults upon females; buggery appears to relate only to forcible anal penetration of the male. Despite the existence on the stature books of the crime of non-consensual buggery, the category of rape, historically defined as non-consensual penetration of the vagina by a penis, has been extended to apply to males. Even so, it hardly appears to be the same offence, for the first case tried resulted in a life sentence for attempted male rape, a circumstance unheard of in recent times in cases involving a female victim. So what is going on? One way of explaining the contrast is to consider the prevailing notion of the gravity of the offence as predicated upon an implicit judgment of the appropriateness or inappropriateness of the victim.

In 1993, 621 sexual assaults upon males were reported

---

[23] Irma Mackay, 'Educating the professional to aid abuse victims in achieving human rights', *Intimate Violence: Interdisciplinary Perspectives*, ed. Emilio C. Viano (Washington, DC: Hemisphere, 1992); L. Macleod, *Wife battering in Canada: The Vicious Circle* (Hull, Quebec: Canadian Government Publishing Centre, 1980).

[24] See e.g. S. A. and J. B. McConahay, 'Sexual permissiveness, sex-role rigidity, and violence across cultures', *Journal of Social Issues*, **33** (1977); M. R. Burt, 'Cultural myths and supports for rape', *Journal of Personality and Social Psychology*, **38** (1980); J. V. P. Check and N. M. Malamuth, 'Sex role stereotyping and reactions to depictions of stranger versus acquaintance rape', *Journal of Personality and Social Psychology*, **45** (1983).

compared with 3,639 sexual assaults upon females. Of these, three of the sexual assaults on males were allegedly perpetrated by females together with thirty-four of the assaults on women. There were moreover 1,704 reported rapes; three of the alleged perpetrators, strangely, were female and were all committed for trial. This figure compares with 371 reported cases of non-consensual buggery. There are some crimes that can only be committed by men, such as soliciting by men (208 reported cases) and indecent exposure (854 cases) and indecency between men (540 cases). Women, on the other hand, are the only perpetrators of infanticide. It is clear in looking at such statistics that it is all a matter of words. Of naming. To alter names is to alter fact.

Catherine Mackinnon has memorably described the progression from life into law

You learn that language does not belong to you, that you cannot use it to say what you know, that knowledge is not what you learn from your life, that information is not made out of your experience.[25]

The woman who encounters sexual violence will find, if she dares to protest, that she will be seen not as an offended party but as the corpus delicti, a piece of evidence. She is, as it were the thing stolen; the offence has been committed not against her but against the state. Her perception, that a crime has been committed against her, is irrelevant. What the investigators have to establish is whether she had it coming. Can a man really be blamed for raping this rapable thing? The man who brought the complaint of rape was considered unrapable; the sanctity of his body was the sanctity of the body of the judge himself, but women are permeable, have been penetrated, are for penetration. Possibly more important than pornography in this dynamic is the unremarkable and inexorable opening up of women's bodies by modern medicine. Almost without our noticing it, we have allowed women's

[25] C. MacKinnon, *Only Words* (London, 1994), 3.

bodies to be penetrated more and more casually more and more often; devices are installed in them, cervices are scanned annually, breasts are rendered transparent, pelves should be regularly bimanually palpated, the pregnant pelvis is sounded, images of our innards are projected routinely. It is obvious that men resist such penetration; year after year we are told that men will not, as it were, submit to the doctor. They die of preventable malignancies because they will not submit to the penetration of examination. Their bodies remain obstreperously intact; women's bodies are increasingly permeable. No culture has ever demanded that women's bodies be as routinely and irresponsibly penetrated even in sex as ours does. The connection between intravaginal intercourse and pregnancy was severed precisely in order that the vagina be penetrable without ceremony. Non-penetrative love-play was less and less practised. Only penetration was the real thing. The semiotic contrast between the penetrator and the penetrated is so basic as to be ineradicable. A man who aligns himself with the penetrated will suffer the same fate, and may very well comport himself in the same feminine fashion, as the female sex object. The extent of his mimicry of femininity is the clearest indication of its origin not in biology but in masculinist culture.

It is my contention that this unremarkable, normal contrast between the intact masculine body and the perforated feminine body is as important in furnishing the fantasy imagery of gender interplay as the subliminal representation of women's bodies as merchandise in advertising. The pornography of everyday life is more important in the psychopathology of everyday life than self-defining deviant expressions are. The pornography that matters is the pornography of advertising with its insistent message that anyone who fails to find instant gratification is a loser and a nerd. The phallic imagery of automobile advertising has long been understood; acceleration from 0 to 60 m.p.h. in 2.4 seconds, or whatever, equals automatic erection fantasy.

In a society that runs on subliminal commercial pornography the woman herself is acutely conscious of her status as a thing to rape used; the use to be made of her is portrayed explicitly, implicitly, and subliminally, all around her. In the words of Catherine McKinnon

to survive you learn shame and how to cover it with sexual bravado, inefficacy and how to make it seductive, secrecy and the habit of not telling what you know until you forget it . . . you develop a self who is ingratiating and obsequious and imitative and aggressively passive and silent—you learn, in a word, femininity.[26]

Victimologists have recognized this process

Rooted in a social structure which is characterized by male domination, the socialization processes of the male and female act to mold women into victims and provide the procedure for legitimizing them in this role.[27]

The female eunuch is a person to whom things are done rather than a person who does things. This semiology is what creates the contrast between the treatment of the raped or murdered male and the treatment of the raped or murdered female not only in courts of law but in the media. The unlawful killing of one male by another generally receives less attention than the murder of a woman. A female victim makes national news anywhere in the country where male victims do not. Witnesses at the trial of Rosemary West have been tampered with by the media who have offered them hundreds of thousands of pounds for lurid details precisely because the Gloucester serial murders involve women, young women, and display a pronounced sexual element. The only interest there can be in the photographs of the victims that are republished again and again is in their sex and their youth. Every day throughout the trial the gallery of blurred and by now drearily familiar photographs

---

[26] MacKinnon, 5.
[27] K. Weis and S. S. Borges, 'Victimology and rape: the case of the legitimate victim', *The Rape Victim*, ed. D. R. Nass (Dubuque, IA: Kendall/Hunt, 1977).

was reproduced in all media. On the day after the initial verdict, the *Independent* blazoned the ten faces in colour across the front page. The publishers would say that their intention is to rouse the ire of the public against the monsters who did these women in. In fact, the occasion of a trial like that of Rosemary West provides a legitimate occasion for the most exciting, that is to say, the most revolting kind of pornography.[28] Likewise, every mention of the murder of Naomi Smith repeats the detail that she was a schoolgirl, raising the titillating image of a dead nubile female body in a gymslip.[29] I am less concerned with the probability that some men are clipping such news reports and hiding them in their sock drawer, than I am with the insidious effect that this kind of media caressing of such stories must have on women themselves. What is being disseminated is a stereotyped image of women as creatures to be violated and destroyed. In creating the atmosphere in which women fear death at the hands of men and men do not, though they are more likely to die at the hands of men, this mechanism is of overriding importance.

Given such a culture how can women struggle towards being victims no longer, seeing themselves as victims no longer, correcting the astigmatism that shows them their own image as victims?

Caring agencies want, even need, to see the woman as a victim; however, the woman may want, or need, to believe that she is not a victim, in order to survive. She may tell herself that her partner bashes her because he loves her. She

---

[28] In the particular instance other women who had been abused by the Wests were forced to re-enact and elaborate their experiences verbally, i.e. to generate the pornographic text themselves, in an atmosphere of the most fervid interest. This was followed by the unforced admissions of a daughter of Frederick West, given in vividly remembered and relentlessly recounted detail on prime time television. Shock and disgust must have been occasioned by her disclosures, but there was also intense interest amounting to excitement.

[29] McKinnon has convincingly made the case for the cross-examination of the victim in rape trials functioning as titillation. See also Jane Caputi, *The Age of Sex Crime* (Bowling Green, OH: Bowling Green University Popular Press, 1987), 8.

may blame herself for being sexually unresponsive or remiss in carrying out her allotted tasks. If the relationship is to survive she must see a way of improving the situation; to recognize aggression as the expression of innate violence and hatred is to conclude that abandoning the relationship is the only option. In begging a woman to prosecute a brutalizing partner we are asking her to abandon her considerable emotional investment. From a feminist point of view we might want to encourage greater 'victimization' in the sense of persuading women to feel more outrage at family violence and to demand redress. Historically, the amount of violence women are prepared to accept in a family context has diminished; a husband is no longer accorded the right physically to chastise his wife. Wife-beating is understood to be a crime, but a crime that usually goes unpunished. General population surveys show that women beaten by their partners report about 10 per cent of the violent incidents they have been involved in. Women at lesser risk of repeated assault may be more willing to report the incident. The likelihood of arrest and prosecution following reporting ranges from 12 to 50 per cent and the inevitability of the enraged partner's even more enraged return is a powerful deterrent. Victimization studies outline risk-taking and poor judgement as factors in crime precipitation, as well as frequenting a dangerous environment and remaining in contact with perpetrators. The battered wife is guilty on all counts.

However, in the feminist analysis of rape and sexual assault the idea of victimization is further developed as the victim's *taking the blame* for the act. Women who have been raped are expected to feel ashamed, dirty, and so forth. The decision to allow women alleging rape to remain anonymous in courts of law actually reinforces this tendency. In my view it places the angry female victim on the same footing as children; it both emphasizes her vulnerability and depersonalizes her. I am particularly concerned with the woman's own perception of the crime against herself, the damage she has suffered, and its consequences for her future development and life career. One of the questions, put crudely, is whether a rapist is responsible for his victim's nightmares or inability to endure intimacy or whether she herself is cooperating with him in devastating herself.

There is a lamentable tendency in contemporary discussions of crime and punishment to assume that the punishment for a crime should be adequate to assuage the feelings of the injured parties, which is accompanied by a tendency of the injured parties to consider that their interests are best served by baying for blood. Even in the recent sad case of the death by misadventure of Leah Betts, public ire was directed against an imaginary individual, the evil pusher who sold Leah the Ecstasy tablet. Vindictiveness, in my view, is itself an aspect of victimization, understood in my sense as maximization of the offence or damage delimitation. In my definition, victimization is what happens when an injured party allows the offence to take over her life.

In the case of femicide clearly the offence does take over the victim's life in that it takes her life; in the case of homicide victimization in its classic sense is continued in the law court by the defence which must in the defendant's interest present the victim as co-perpetrator. In the case of female victims this is still astonishingly easy to do. When the murderer and his victim are of the same sex, victimization requires proof that the dead man struck the first blow; when the murdered person is a woman it is sufficient to prove that she spoke out of turn. The woman herself being dead, the murder process is perpetuated by the assassination of her character. As much as criminologists may deplore 'blaming the victim' it is still the staple of the defence in cases of women killed by their sexual partners.[30]

[30] Sue Lees, 'Naggers, whores and libbers: provoking men to kill', *Femicide: The Politics of Woman-Killing*, ed. J. Radford and Diana H. Russell (Birmingham: Open University Press, 1992).

There is little that the criminal law can do to assist women in making their way out of the victim stereotype, out of perceiving themselves as quarry for male predation, but a radical reform of the law on sex offences would make a contribution if, and only if, it degendered the victim. Although I still believe that the separate category of rape should be abolished as a piece of historic baggage based in the rights of males over women and a continuation of the magnification of the harmless necessary penis into a weapon of destruction, it is clear to me that merely rearranging the old offences under new names has had little effect in improving the status of the victim in the courts or out of them. Judges have simply imposed the old tariffs and imposed the same burden of proof that they did before the nomenclature was changed. Reporting, investigation, prosecution, and success rates have not notably improved and women have spent more time and energy in acting out the victim role over months and months than ever before. A more important initial step would be to draft a criminal law of sexual assault in which the sex of the victim was unspecified and in which the emphasis was less upon the genitals of the attacker than upon the genitals of the victim, as it were, in order to place the role of the penis in something like a realistic ranking with other offensive instruments. The Director of the Cambridge Institute of Criminology put the case like this, about fifteen years ago, speaking of the Nebraskan law:

This type of definition gets rid of awkward distinctions based on the gender of victim and assailant, whether the assault was heterosexual or homosexual, and unrealistic distinctions between oral, anal and vaginal intrusions. In my view more realistic legal distinctions could and should be made between sexual crimes that are truly heinous and those that are less so. This in no way contradicts the justice of the feminist claim that women should have the fullest possible legal protection from annoyance, molestation or assault. However the presence of the maximum penalty of life imprisonment for any but the most serious of sexual crimes is a hindrance rather than a protection, since it means that the accused is desperate to defend himself at any cost and the jury have to feel extremely sure before they record a verdict of guilty.[31]

This opinion was not respected by the committee that agreed the amendments to the British criminal law. The life sentence was allowed to stand. And it has since been handed down, not for a case of rape involving a female victim but for an attempted rape on a male. Rather than clarification, the new amendments have brought further confusion. Deliberations about consent have been made no easier and the inconsistency of judgments has brought the law into further disrepute. The criminal law does not exist to protect but to punish the injured; there is nothing in the present situation to reassure women that they will be believed if they complain— recent studies have shown that police still spend a good deal of energy trying to sniff out malicious reports and an astonishingly high proportion of women withdraw their complaints, not because they were malicious but because they could see that their case was hopeless.[32]

The most hopeful development by far has been the bringing of civil cases by women for damages from the men who assaulted them. Angry women have stood up and pointed the finger at the man who humiliated, outraged, and injured them and been believed. What this process requires is the opposite of anonymity. The plaintiff takes action as herself rather than the patriarchal state taking action in its own interest. She is not an anonymous Exhibit A but an agent in her own interest. The defendant is entitled to bring evidence of precipitation of the offence in mitigation, but he cannot thereby succeed in denying the offence altogether. In the civil court the offended woman faces her assailant as an equal, using the

---

[31] Donald J. West, 'The victim's contribution to sexual offences', *Perspectives on Rape and Sexual Assault*, ed. June Hopkins (London: Harper & Row, 1984) 14.

[32] Susan Carnyella-Macdonald, 'An assessment of rape reform: victim and case treatment under Michigan's model', *International Review of Victimology*, 3 (1991).

law as she is entitled to do rather than the law using her in its own interest. The women who have had the courage and endurance to see this process through are heroines; their success should show the criminal law just how radically it must reform if it is to neutralize the prevailing impression that females are appropriate victims.

6

Raising Darwin's Consciousness: Sexual Selection and the Prehominid Origins of Patriarchy

SARAH BLAFFER HRDY

Was she beautiful or not beautiful?
George Eliot, *Daniel Deronda*, 1876

Why would a primate require beauty in his mate?

Herbert Spencer once described the novelist George Eliot as 'the most admirable woman, mentally, I ever met . . .'. In his autobiography Spencer noted that 'the greatness of her intellect conjoined with her womanly qualities and manner, generally keep me by her side most of the evening' (1904: 457).

Admiration was mutual. In an 1852 letter which ended

I thank Robert May, Susan Iversen, and Colin Blakemore for their role in revisiting the 'woman question' in a series of lectures dedicated to Herbert Spencer. I thank Nick Davies, Bill Hamilton, Alexander Harcourt, Kim Hill, Daniel Hrdy, Doug Jones, Debra Judge, Jane Lancaster, Amy Parish, Kelly Stewart, and Carol Worthman for critical discussion, help with references, for sharing preprints of work in press, and Dietrich von Bothmer for sharing with me his wealth of knowledge about ancient Greek vase paintings. In addition, I owe a large debt to Nancy Paxton for her analysis of Eliot's relationship with Spencer, to Mary Jane West-Eberhard's for her work on flexible phenotypes, and to Patricia Gowaty for inspiration of several sorts. My indebtedness to these scholars for causing me to think along new lines is greater than can be adequately conveyed here. A version of this lecture, originally delivered at Oxford on December 4, 1995, was published in *Human Nature 8* (1): 1–49 (1997).

provocatively: 'I suppose no woman ever before wrote such a letter as this—but I am not ashamed of it, for I am conscious that in the light of reason and true refinement I am worthy of your respect and tenderness, whatever gross men or vulgar-minded women might think of me', Eliot confided. 'If you become attached to someone else, then I must die, but until then, I could gather courage to work and make life valuable, if only I had you near me. I do not ask you to sacrifice anything—I would be very good and cheerful and never annoy you. But I find it impossible to contemplate life under any other conditions' (Haight, vol. 8: 57; Karl 1995: 142–7; esp. Paxton 1991).

But Spencer—who died a bachelor—turned her down, reputedly because he was convinced that the natural function of woman is to be beautiful, which Eliot was not. As Spencer later, somewhat ruefully, wrote (Eliot was by now contentedly paired with their friend, George Lewes): 'Physical beauty is a *sine qua non* with me; as was once unhappily proved where the intellectual traits and the emotional traits were of the highest '(Spencer 1904, vol. II: 445). Spencer believed that 'Nature's . . . supreme end, is the welfare of posterity', and was convinced that 'as far as posterity is concerned, a cultivated intelligence based upon a bad physique is of little worth, seeing that its descendants will die out in a generation or two' (Spencer 1858: 395, cited in Paxton 1991: 33).

Some of Spencer's late twentieth-century successors are similarly focused on female beauty, and convinced that they have discovered a 'species-typical' universal male preference, insisting that: 'Beautiful young women are sexually attractive to men because beauty and youth are closely linked with fertility and reproductive value. In evolutionary history, males who were able to identify and mate with fertile females had the greatest reproductive success . . .'. (Buss 1994*b*: caption to Fig. 7, showing teenage girls in a dating bar).

As David Buss (1994*b*) points out: 'A fourteen year-old woman has a higher reproductive value than a 24 year-old woman, because her *future* contribution to the gene pool is higher on average ...'. Along with symmetry and other indices of past and current developmental health (Thornhill and Thornhill 1993; Thornhill and Gangestad 1996), researchers have documented preferences for neotenous, or 'baby-faced' features, particularly, large eyes, small nose and ears, large brow relative to chin ('high ratio of neurocranial to lower-facial features': Jones 1995), and more reduced vertical dimensions than the average face of an adult female (McArthur and Berry 1983; Riedl 1990; and esp. Jones 1995).

To a primatologist, such preferences must be puzzling. There is not a shred of evidence for any other primate that youth, neoteny, or specific body ratios considered indicative of reproductive value—all commonly cited indices of a woman's 'desirability' (e.g. Jones and Hill 1993; Singh 1993)—affect male willingness to mate. Instead, for every monkey or ape species for which information on male preferences is available, priority is given to fully adult, multiparous females who are signalling probable ovulation (Anderson 1986). Even in those monkey and ape species where adolescent females exhibit unusually large or 'exaggerated' sexual swellings, full adult males rarely choose to copulate with them, and they mate instead with subadult, subordinate males (Anderson and Bielert 1994: 288).

Consider the case of Jane Goodall's famous 'Old Flo'. Tattered and misshapen by life's insults, Flo, fully swollen at midcycle, was peerless in her attractiveness to locally dominant males (Goodall 1971). Based on records for 166 wild chimpanzees at Gombe, primatologist Caroline Tutin (1975) was able to study male criteria for mate selection whenever two females happened to be maximally tumescent on the same day. 'On 30 of 38 occasions, the older female was selected' (Tutin 1975: 165 and 256). Excluding eight cases involving young adult males, the full adult males chose the older female 90 per cent of the time. Tutin attributes chimp preferences to the greater fecundability and maternal experience of parous females.

In Flo's case, even more would have been at stake. This redoubtable old female's range was nestled deep within territorial boundaries patrolled by Flo's older sons (several of whom became high-ranking males at Gombe), and their fathers, and this familiar and productive larder eventually passed to Flo's daughter Fifi, a female who—instead of migrating at puberty as do most other female chimps—managed to stay on near Flo, eventually inheriting her mother's range and producing there six healthy offspring, the Gombe record for female reproductive success (Wallis and Almasi 1995; Wallis 1995: pers. comm.). Reproductively speaking, male preferences for old Flo were well placed: matings with Flo were fertile and daughters and sons born to her survived to maturity, and became successful breeders in their own right.

Across primates (including humans), young females are characterized by adolescent subfertility, or, if conception does occur, are more prone to pregnancy failure (reviewed in Lancaster 1986; Anderson and Bielert 1994). More importantly, across virtually all primate species, infants born to first-time mothers suffer higher rates of infant mortality than do offspring born to experienced, parous females (Drickamer 1974; Glander 1980; Silk *et al.* 1981). Clearly, it makes evolutionary sense for males to select females not only on the basis of fecundity, but also based on their probability of producing offspring that survive. When intergenerational effects are likely to be important, males should also take into account female status, kin ties, or home range quality.

Given these realities, why would male *Homo sapiens*, virtually unique among primates, be so attracted to neotenous traits? Surely such preferences do not derive from the greater fecundability of young females, where fecundability is defined as the probability that a female will become pregnant over the course of a year of unprotected intercourse. For fourteen-year-old girls are higher in future potential reproductive value, but *not* more likely to become pregnant than twenty-four-year-olds (Lancaster 1986; Wood 1994: esp. fig.

2.9). Rather, such preferences derive from uniquely human institutions whereby men in many societies do not merely *mate* with virginal and compliant young females, but *acquire* them as wives, concubines, or slaves, whom they essentially 'own', and as a consequence, in many societies are also obliged to provide for long term.[1] Whereas in every other primate, males and females provide for themselves, in our own species, male desire to 'own' women is apparently great enough for men to undertake to provide for them. From the Code of Hammurabi (probably the first fully fledged codification for a patriarchal system) onwards, for example, patriarchal marriages guaranteed maintenance for discarded or superseded wives, as well as widows (Lerner 1986: 106–8, 265, n. 20). But when marriage or 'ownership' of women is not an option, as for example, when men are not in a position to monopolize resources mothers need for offspring, I predict men will select from healthy mates on the basis of fertility indices (e.g., signs of maturity and adequate fat deposits to sustain pregnancy and lactation and/or the stability of the woman's resource base) rather than depending on how young or neotenous the woman appears.

Note that the sole non-human primate exception is *Papio hamadryas,* a bizarre desert-adapted species where young males build up a permanent harem by kidnapping juvenile females from their mothers, and rearing them to adulthood. *Papio hamadryas* is the only non-human primate in which both other males, and females themselves, behave as if that male 'owned' her. Wherever she goes, he watches; if she

[1] As Doug Jones (1995) points out, menopause may make it especially important for human males to avoid acquiring females approaching the end of their reproductive careers. But even assuming women live long enough to reach menopause, one does not need a preference for neotenous traits in order to accomplish this. Attention to hair colour, skin tone, or breast shape make excellent indices. Prior to cosmetics, dyes, and plastic surgery, such women who survived long enough to reach menopause would be qualitatively rather than quantitatively different from fertile women. As for older women whose fecundity is beginning to decline but who are still capable of conceiving, their condition would be of little relevance to male mating decisions unless the man sought to acquire her as his property to hold long term—which is my point.

strays, he herds her by biting the back of her neck. Out of some 175 species of primate, *P. hamadryas* is the only one where the old-fashioned primatological term 'harem'— employed by Hans Kummer the first time he ever saw a group of these monkeys at the Zurich zoo, and later retained by him when he described them in his classic monograph— actually applies.

Patriarchy viewed as a construct to control female sexuality

> We don't ask what a woman does—we ask whom she belongs to . . .
>
> George Eliot, *Mill on the Floss*, 1860

According to Gerda Lerner's broad definition, patriarchy refers to 'the manifestation and institutionalization of male dominance over women and children in the family and the extension of male dominance over women in society in general. It implies that men hold power in all the important institutions of society and that women are deprived of access to such power. It does *not* imply that women are either totally powerless or totally deprived of rights, influence and resources' (1986: 29). I also concur with Lerner that patriarchy predates classical antiquity but whereas she would date its origins in historical time, around the third millennium BC, I have insisted that its origins must be far older (Hrdy 1981: 9; see also Smuts 1995).

Following the Marxist theorist Friedrich Engels, feminist historians have traced the origins of human patriarchal marriage as male-dominated family structures expanded to include male authority and customary male control over both property and labour. Rarely, however, are we permitted more than sketchy glimpses of this early patriarchal history where men not only dominate, but own, women.

The capture of women was a primary objective of early warfare (Spencer 1885; Lerner 1986), and it was under such circumstances during the Trojan war, that the Greek warrior Achilles obtained his beautiful concubine Briseis. A Greek vase painting by Makron in 480 BC depicts Agamemnon, commander in chief of the Greek army, commandeering Achilles' prize (Fig. 6.1). Although at first awarded to Achilles, Briseis was subsequently reclaimed by his commander—the source of Achilles' wrath at the outset of the *Iliad*. The painting depicts Agamemnon leading Briseis, holding her by the wrist, in the time-honoured gesture of the bridegroom or, in this instance, signalling ownership of a trophy of war—origin of the current term, not then a joke, 'trophy wife'.

Serendipitously, three independent interpretations of this scene from the opening of the *Iliad* depicting life in Homer's Greece are laid out for us, first by Engels (1884: 126) and then, a century later, by sociobiologist Matt Ridley (1993:

FIG. 6.1. Agamemnon holds Briseis by the wrist, which is the time honoured gesture of a bridegroom leading his bride, denoting both 'taking possession' and the marriage union. From an Attic red-figured skyphos attributed to Makron, and signed by Hieron as potter on one handle. (Permission needed from the Louvre.)

205) and finally by feminist historian Gerda Lerner (1986: 84). Each examines the question of why men captured women by citing the quarrel over Briseis.

At issue (in Ridley's words) is 'Agamemnon's insistence on confiscating a concubine, Briseis, from Achilles in compensation for (Agamemnon) having to give back his concubine, Chryseis to her priest-father . . .' (Ridley 1993: 205). Ridley and Engels had no doubts that 'In Homer young women are booty and are handed over to the pleasure of the conquerors, the handsomest being picked by the commanders in order of rank . . . (and) these girls were also taken back to Greece and brought under the same roof as the wife . . .', sons begotten from them becoming freemen and receiving a small share of the paternal inheritance (Engels 1884: 126). On this point both follow Darwin: 'women are the constant cause of war both between members of the same tribe and between distinct tribes . . .', and 'The strongest party always carries off the prize' (Darwin 1871: 556–7).

Feminist Lerner concurs, save on one point: 'After Agamemnon carries out his threat and acquires Briseis by force, which causes Achilles to sulk in his tent and withdraw from the battle, the king does not touch her. He in fact *does not actually want her* but wanted to win a point of honour against Achilles—a fine example of the reification of women . . .' (my italics). For Lerner, 'the meaning of the enslavement of women (is) to win status and honour among men' (Lerner 1986: 84).[2]

Normally viewed as antagonists, a Marxist, a feminist and a sociobiologist[3] concur that men seek to control women, and,

---

[2] This same discrepancy surfaces in feminist versus sociobiological interpretations for rape. For feminists, rape is a 'process of intimidation', essentially an act of domination with primarily symbolic intent, while for sociobiologists, it represents an act of domination with a primarily *reproductive* intent. Compare, for example, Susan Brownmiller (1975) on rape with the sociobiological analysis by Thornhill and Thornhill (1983).

[3] For the non-Engelian, purportedly Marxist view that 'we are the being whose essence lies in having no essence . . .', see Stephen Jay Gould (1976) on biological potential vs. biological determinism. For the view that 'The sexism in sociobiology is an outgrowth of the theory itself . . .', see Alper *et al.* (1978). For

to a lesser extent, they concur on why patriarchal systems (under certain conditions[4]) emerge: a perceived need by males to control female sexuality, and in Engels' words to 'produce children of undisputed paternity'. An obscure feminist pamphlet—the kind passed out on American sidewalks in the early 1970s—summarizes important areas of agreement

In patriarchal cultures like the one we were all brought up in, sexuality is a crucial issue. Beyond all the symbolic aspects of the sexual act (symbolizing the male's dominance, manipulation and control over the female), it assumes an overwhelming practical importance. . . . Under normal circumstances it is agreed that a man is needed to provide sperm to the conception of the baby, but it is practically impossible to determine *which* man. The only way a man can be absolutely sure that he is the one to have contributed that sperm is to control the sexuality of the woman. . . . He may keep her separate from any other man as in a harem, he may threaten her with violence

more on feminist critiques of sociobiology see Hubbard *et al.* (1979). Masters (1982, p. 288) provides an interesting explanation for sociobiology becoming erroneously equated with 'conservative' points of view: '. . . the Marxist theory of human history is, par excellence, a systemic or "sociological" one. In contrast to the social contract approach of Anglo-Saxon liberalism . . . Marxism denies the possibility of deriving social attitudes from the interests or "rights" of isolated individuals . . .'. For replies to feminist critics of sociobiology, see Liesen (1995).

[4] There has been a tendency among scholars from Bachofen to Gimbutas to confuse a widespread fascination with female sexuality manifested in figurines termed 'fertility goddesses' unearthed across large areas of the Ancient Near East and Early Europe, with evidence of female political power. Even Engels, as well as modern historians like Gerda Lerner, assumed that at one time humans passed through matriarchal, or at least matrilineal and matrilocal phases with considerable equality between the sexes, before becoming patrilineal, patrilocal, and more or less male-dominated. This may have been the case in some instances. However, there is no necessary social progression from matriarchy, patriarchy, to, finally, egalitarian societies. The task that lies before social scientists is to identify those ecological, demographic, and historical conditions that contribute to the development of particular family systems. However, specifying the ecological conditions under which patrilineal and patrilocal social systems develop in hunter-gathering, herding, and horticultural economies, and specifying the inheritance and other customs that cause paternity certainty to become a paramount concern for patrilines are complex tasks, beyond the scope of this essay. These topics are discussed preliminarily in Hrdy and Judge (1993) and will be dealt with in greater depth elsewhere (Hrdy 1999).

if she strays, he may devise a mechanical method of preventing inter-course like a chastity belt, he may remove her clitoris to decrease her erotic impulses, or he may convince her that sex is the same thing as love and if she has sexual relations with anyone else, she is violating the sacred ethics of love ... (Marval 1971)[5]

Note that the main difference between arguments made by feminists like Lerner and those made by sociobiologists, is that these feminists view male dominance as an historical construction as illustrated in the dispute between Agamemnon and Achilles. Male dominance is a socially constructed end in its own right. As Lerner puts it: 'Patriarchy is a historic creation formed by men and women in a process which took nearly 2,500 years to its completion. ... The basic unit of its organization was the patriarchal family which both expressed and constantly generated its rules and values ...'. (Lerner 1986: 212). By contrast, sociobiologists (and to some extent feminists like Marval, as well, for there is no strict dichotomy here) assume that the ultimate goal of male domination is reproductive success, and they identify sexual selection—rather than male desire for power—as the engine driving the system (Dickemann 1979, 1981; Hrdy 1981; Smuts 1995). Instead of third millennium BC Mesopotamia, an evolutionary perspective pushes the search for patriarchy's origins back in time by millions of years by asking an additional question: *why* should males seek to control females?

Why should males attempt to control females?

Should the hypothesis be true that one of the requisite cornerstones upon which all modern civilization were founded was *coercive* suppression of women's inordinate sexuality, one looks back over the long history of women and their relationship to men, children, and

---

[5] Cited by Hite (1976: 151) and Hrdy (1981: 178), I have been unable to learn more about the author or to trace the development of her views, but think it likely that Marval's views derive from Sherfey's 1966 essay. It is hoped that feminist historians of science will pursue some of these leads.

society since the Neolithic revolution with a deeper, almost awesome sense of ironic tragedy.

Mary Jane Sherfey (1966)

Darwin's innately 'coy' females. As conceived by Darwin, sexual selection involves two processes: 'competition between individuals of the same sex, generally the males, in order to drive away or kill their rivals, the females remaining passive' and mate choice, being competition 'between individuals of the same sex in order to excite or charm those of the opposite sex generally the females' who are no longer passive (Darwin 1871: 239, 256–8; for valuable overviews of Darwin's ideas on female choice see Small 1989 and Cronin 1991). Guided by a theory that was not only very powerful but largely correct, Darwin had an uncanny knack for separating the anecdotal chaff from the true kernels of natural history reaching him from all corners of the globe, but when it came to females, and especially female choice, his vision was impaired by the blinkers of Victorian prejudice.

Accustomed to the country gentry among whom he lived, familiar with medical opinions of the day to the effect that 'the majority of women (happily for them) are not much troubled with sexual feelings of any kind' (Acton 1865: 112–13), Darwin concurred with contemporary nineteenth-century wisdom about women. According to Darwin: 'The female ... with the rarest exception, is less eager (to copulate) than the male ... she generally 'requires to be courted'; she is coy, and may often be seen endeavouring for a long time to escape from the male ...' (Darwin 1871: 273).

'Coyness', Darwin believed, was part of a universal female strategy to ensure that she only mates with the best locally available male. Clearly, if this assumption was correct, males would not need to curtail the sexuality of a mate who had specifically selected just him.

Darwin's working assumptions might have been different had he been working out sexual selection theory three centuries earlier. By 1594, in what can be regarded as the first adventure novel to be written in the English language, Thomas Nashe's *The Unfortunate Traveller*, the ape had become a symbol for a wife's 'unconstant wantonness . . .' (Janson 1952: chapter IX and esp. 280, n. 41). Although Darwin was clearly familiar with sexual swellings in the perineal region, he apparently never had the opportunity to observe the twelve-day period around a female chimpanzee's maximal tumescence, when she typically mates about one to four times an hour with thirteen or more partners. Over her lifetime, a female chimpanzee will copulate around six thousand times (Wrangham 1993) resulting in, at most, six living offspring (Fifi's record).

Surely it was Darwin's presumption that females hold themselves in reserve for the best available male (as do female bison or pronghorn antelopes) that left him puzzled by sexual swellings. Somehow, their obvious function of advertising female readiness to mate was not obvious to him. 'No case', he confessed, 'interested and perplexed me so much as the brightly coloured hinder ends and adjoining parts of certain monkeys' (Darwin 1876: 18–19).[6]

Although appropriate for many animals, the appellation 'coy'—which has remained unchallenged dogma for the succeeding hundred years—did not then, and does not today, apply to the observed behaviour of monkey and ape females at mid-cycle.[7] Instead, I would argue that sexual 'coyness',

[6] In this brief 1876 note, Darwin actually starts with a question about anogenital coloration generally, but then is diverted from the larger question of why sexual swellings and coloration exist, to explain why they exist in males, mimicking female swellings and colorations at mid-cycle and during the breeding season. That is, in his only publication specifically devoted to sexual coloration in monkeys, Darwin focuses on males and the possibility that sexual swellings in *males* might (like the peacock's tail) have evolved in order to attract females.

[7] Hrdy (1986) traces through time the view that 'there is nearly always a combination of an undiscriminating eagerness in the males and a discriminating passivity in the females . . .' (Bateman 1948: 365), as this stereotype is picked up from Bateman and passed on via Trivers (1972) and Daly and Wilson (1983)—some of the best evolutionary biologists of our time—into contemporary evolutionary dogma. So compelling is this stereotype of 'urgent males and coy females' that it persists, even in a recent book seeking to document that human females create an arena for sperm competition by engaging in extra-pair copulations (Baker and Bellis 1995: esp. sect. w.3.2 and 8ff.). Under 'coyness' in the book index the entry reads: 'See: females'.

extreme discretion, and a concern for 'reputation' found in so many women today derives not from prehuman 'lower origins', as Darwin supposed, but rather from the tens of thousands of years hominid females have been socialised, exchanged between social groups, reproduced, and died (some sooner than others) in various permutations of the patrilocal (or, in ethological parlance, 'male philopatric') patrilineal breeding systems that eventually gave rise in places like the Ancient Near East to fully fledged patriarchy.

Given that Sherfey's book *The Nature and Evolution of Female Sexuality* is the first book of its kind, it seems odd that this book is so rarely cited in the current crop of books about the *evolution* of human sexuality. In the words of evolutionary psychologist Donald Symons, her work is simply 'not taken seriously' (Symons 1979: 91). When Symons—who is about the only evolutionist to cite her—does so, it is to debunk her notion of females whose capacity for multiple orgasms suggests to Sherfey that 'women's inordinate orgasmic capacity did not evolve for monogamous, sedentary cultures' (Sherfey 1966: 37). For Symons, wittier than he is generous, writes: Sherfey's 'sexually insatiable woman is to be found primarily, if not exclusively, in the ideology of feminism, the hopes of boys, and the fears of men'. Even a favourable mention of Sherfey is liable to invite derision (Symons 1982).

Yet Sherfey herself displayed considerable insight into the predicament created by her dual identity as scientist and feminist. She ended her book with the mythological tale of Tiresias, the only living mortal to have experienced life as both male and female. Outraged because Tiresias had revealed the

---

Interestingly, the word 'coy' appears to derive from an old French word for 'quiet'—hence reserved—or else from the word 'coy' to describe a cage or a hollow trap for ducks (hence, decoys?). Possibly then current usage, which refers to a creature who holds herself in reserve while possibly flirting or enticing, reflects some conflation of these old meanings. Nevertheless, like my colleague Helena Cronin, 'I can't resist wondering if males were choosey about mates, would they be described as "coy"—or discriminating, judicious, responsible prudent, discerning?' (1991: 248).

depths of female sexual sensations, the goddess Hera struck him blind.

Sherfey was laying out her arguments in the early 1960s, before primatologists knew much about sexual behaviour in wild primates, certainly before we guessed at the existence of orgasmic capacity in non-human females. Yet some of her hunches hit close to the mark. The work contains errors in scholarly judgement (e.g. Sherfey gives too much weight to skimpy evidence supposedly documenting sexually libertarian matriarchies), and other problems. Yet, returning to this subject after a hiatus of fifteen years, I am struck by how insightful Sherfey's central premise was: patriarchal social organization *was* partially an outgrowth of male counter-strategies for controlling the primate legacy of an assertive female sexuality of *prehominid* origin.

I regret that Sherfey—whose work was initially so very controversial, and then largely forgotten—did not live to see some of her guesses validated by those studying the sexual behaviour of female primates (Wallen 1990, 1995; Slob *et al.* 1986, 1991; Hrdy 1981 and others). Female sexuality among anthropoid primates (as Sherfey suspected) *is* qualitatively and quantitatively different from many of the mammals that Darwin would have been most familiar with. Sherfey's early proposal—that 'the satiation-in-insatiation state may have been an important factor in the adaptive radiation of the primates leading to man—and a major barrier to the evolution of modern man . . .' (Sherfey 1966: 144) was both rashly overstated and also visionary.

To understand either the evolution of the primate sexual swellings that so perplexed Darwin, or to understand the evolutionary *and historical* pressures that would lead to patriarchy, requires us to set aside the old assumption that female primates evolved to select and mate with a single best male. Rather, anthropoid females were selected to—in one way or another—ensure that they mate with a range of male partners.

Among most mammals, mating is strictly confined to the period of 'heat' at ovulation. For a sow in oestrus, just an aerosol whiff of testicular steroids from the androgen-laden saliva of a boar, combined with pressure on her back, are sufficient to induce the immobilization response in which the female stands still to be mounted (Izard 1983). Among prosimian primates, such as galagos, an epithelial membrane seals the vagina except for a 48-hour window at ovulation, rendering mating at other times impossible (Doyle 1974; Lipschitz 1992).

Among anthropoid primates, however, female sexual receptivity is less circumscribed. Imagine a continuum ranging from the strictly circumscribed receptivity of galagos to females who like humans, are more facultatively receptive, capable (if not desirous) of engaging in sex on any day of the menstrual cycle. Monkeys and apes fall all along this continuum. In those monkey and ape species that advertise the period around ovulation with oedematous pink swellings in the perineal region, as savanna baboons and chimpanzees do, females usually confine matings to a period of a week or so around the middle of the menstrual cycle, near ovulation. But differences between individuals, and between species, yield many exceptions.

Chimpanzees, for example, restrict matings to mid-cycle but may exhibit a rarely expressed *capacity* to also mate outside of this internally defined endocrinological window. Under some conditions, the sexual skin may swell or deflate in response to social conditions. Ninety-six per cent of 1,475 matings observed at Gombe over a five-year period involved maximally swollen or almost fully swollen females; the remaining copulations involved partially swollen females, except for an idiosyncratic twenty copulations where females lacked detectable swellings (Goodall 1986: 445).

This rarely expressed potential (albeit expressed slightly more in captive than in wild *Pan troglodytes*), is strongly expressed in *Pan paniscus*. Bonobos may exhibit sexual swellings for over 50 per cent of cycle days in the wild (swellings lasting anywhere from three to twenty-two days of a 38-day cycle), or as much as 75 per cent of the cycle in captivity, with copulations occurring at a low level throughout the period of swellings, possibly peaking in frequency when swellings are maximally firm. According to the Japanese primatologist Furuichi, duration of such swellings among wild bonobos in Zaire are influenced by social factors. Prolonged swellings are frequently observed in newly immigrant females, or when the group is in a 'state of high social tension' (Dahl *et al.* 1991; Furuichi 1992).

In primates without sexual swellings, some females lapse from any obviously cyclical pattern, exhibiting prolonged spurts of sexual proceptivity lasting several weeks or more, as in Japanese macaques or African vervet monkeys. Even in species that are normally cyclical, like howler monkeys in the forests of Venezuela, or normally monogamous gibbons, who exhibit only infrequent periods of sexual activity, specific circumstances, such as encounters with unfamiliar males from outside the group, precipitate these lapses (van Noordwijk 1985; Andelman 1987; Takahata 1980; Palombit 1992 esp. appendix C on 'Extra pair copulations in Ketambe siamangs'; for additional cases see review by Hrdy and Whitten 1987).

Regardless of how frequent situation-dependent (as opposed to strictly cyclical) matings are, there is a tendency for female-initiated sexual behaviour to increase at mid-cycle. Among rhesus macaques, where breeding in the wild is typically confined to discrete intervals during specific months of the breeding season, the perineum reddens, but there is no clear-cut visual signal at ovulation. Female attractiveness to males, as well as proceptivity, can be observed all through the follicular phase (especially in captive situations), peaking at mid-cycle, and then subsiding in the luteal phase (Wilson *et al.* 1982, reviewed in Wallen 1990, esp. Fig. 4).

At first blush, human couples who engage in intercourse across the cycle would appear to be exceptional. However, a range of studies involving both heterosexual and homosexual women living in both Western and tribal settings, both in and out of stable relationships, where researchers focused on *female-initiated* sexual interactions and female self-reports about mood changes, found peaks in libido around mid-cycle. Erotic fantasies, feelings of restlessness (attached pedometers measured how far women walked), likelihood of self-stimulation through masturbation, and probability that sexual behaviour will culminate in orgasm—all of these rise around mid-cycle (Table 6.1). Prospective data covering 4,433 cycles taken from 590 women who were monitoring both changes in body temperature and mood, show that sexual desire rises a few days prior to the basal body temperature shift that follows ovulation (Stanislaw and Rice 1988). Not only do women at mid-cycle move about more, as documented in Morris and Udry (1970), but women at mid-cycle exhibit enhanced motor capability, but *not* visual perceptual ability (Hampson and Kimura 1988).

A more in-depth study of a small sample of eight hunter–gatherer women living in the Kalahari, undertaken by anthropologists Carol Worthman, Marj Shostak, and Mel Konner, combined personal interviews with endocrine

TABLE 6.1. *Studies showing increase in female libido at midcyle*

Midcycle Characteristic	References
Female-initiated sex	Adams *et al.* 1978; Matteo and Rissman 1984; Worthman 1978
Female-reported desire or erotic fantasies[†]	Stanislaw and Rice 1988 Adams *et al.* 1978; Grammer 1996
Masturbation	Adams *et al.* 1978
Probability of orgasm	Matteo and Rissman 1984; Worthman 1978

[†] Both Matteo and Rissman's (1984) study of erotic fantasies by women in lesbian relationships, as well as experiments studying female responsiveness to erotic stimuli (such as films; Slob *et al.* 1991), found peaks across the follicular phase of the cycle rather than specifically at midcyle (also see Sanders and Bancroft 1982). Such findings are consistent with nonhuman primate data for macaques (e.g., see Wilson *et al.* 1982 for *Macaca mulatta*).

measures. This study reported statistically significant increases in females reporting 'sexual desire' at mid-cycle. It also documented increased extroversion, and statistically significant increases in likelihood of intercourse with husband during the follicular phase of the cycle, and documented a (non-significant) increase in likelihood of sexual relations with lovers, and a (non-significant) increase in probability of female orgasm at mid-cycle (Worthman 1978, 1988, pers. comm.).

Given these new findings, Sherfey's assessment (1966: 52) that 'sexual responses of women and (other) primates are so nearly identical that the significant differences must have evolved only recently' seems stunningly prescient. The patterning of female sexual desire is far more cyclical than the designation 'continuously receptive' would lead unsuspecting members of our species to believe. At the same time, the cyclical 'oestrous' patterning of sexual behaviour, thought to set other primates apart from humans, reveals more lapses than old dichotomies would lead us to expect. Why?

From Darwin onward, it was assumed that the function of mating was conception, and that sexuality in males and females evolved to ensure insemination—in the female's case, insemination by the best locally available male. In an influential 1976 essay, Clutton-Brock and Harvey proposed that 'by attracting several males', females increase their chances 'of being mated by a relatively high-ranking male', which it almost certainly does. Pursuing this line of argument, Pagel (1994) speculates that sexual swellings result from female–female competition to attract the best male or to ensure fertilization. However, if sperm were in short supply, and fertilization a problem for females, one would expect pressure to be greatest when many females were competing for sperm from just one male. One problem with the argument that sexual swellings evolved to ensure fertilization in a sperm-scarce world is that the majority of species with sexual swellings are found in multi-male rather than uni-male breeding systems—the opposite of what that hypothesis would predict.

TABLE 6.2. *Hypothetical benefits to a female from mating with multiple partners (adapted from Hrdy 1986)*

Genetic Rationales
  1. 'best' male (or alternative to inferior one)
  2. fertility insurance
  3. diverse offspring
  4. generate sperm competition
Nongenetic Processes
  5. female libido an endocrinological by-product
  6. therapeutic benefits
  7. elicit investment or tolerance from 'possible' progenitors
  8. exchange sex for current benefits

But what if in addition to ensuring that a female mate, possibly even that she be inseminated by the best available male, mating also has additional functions not linked to fertilization *per se*? From a male perspective, the 'goal' of mating is to increase the chance that he will fertilize an ovum. But fertilization may be only one of several benefits a female derives from mating, and only one of various selection pressures on her to solicit males. The assumption here is that from the perspective of a female primate, mating has multiple, conceptive *and non-conceptive* functions.

Female primates—especially those with swellings—act as if they are trying to solicit more partners than could possible be necessary to fertilize her. What if, in fact, this is precisely what monkey and ape females have been selected to do? (see Table 6.2)

Assume for a moment that the 'goal' of female sexuality is to motivate females to mate with a range of male partners; how to manage this becomes the 'problem' they must 'solve'. How Old World monkey (Cercopithecoid) and ape (Anthropoid) females solve this problem depends on phylogenetic constraints, current mating system, and local histories.

In multi-male breeding systems, such as baboons and chimpanzees, where a range of males are permanently in residence, the most efficient solution is for females to compress mating into a brief period around ovulation which is signalled by sexual swellings so that males have to follow the female around and compete among themselves for the opportunity to mate, and when it is over, females go back to business-as-usual—foraging.[8]

Sexual swellings have probably evolved independently under multi-male breeding conditions at least three times among catarrhine Old World primates (Dixon 1983). In unimale systems, where the female mates primarily with a single partner but may mate with extra-unit males on an opportunistic basis, there is less likely to be an external sign at ovulation.

Human females constitute an extreme manifestation of this ancient primate potential: females exhibit a mid-cycle peak in libido, but also exhibit a potential for situation-dependent receptivity both at ovulation and at other times as well (under some circumstances, even including during pregnancy) when she happens to encounter outside males. That is, human females are extreme, but scarcely unique.

Female primates solve the 'problem' of mating with a range of males either by concealing ovulation and retaining flexibility to mate opportunistically, or by compressing their mating into a brief period. The former tactic produces monitoring problems for males, the latter produces major competition at the level of sperm. One evolutionary outcome is the now well-documented correlation across primates between testes size and magnitude of polyandrous mating (Harcourt *et al.* 1981) a correlation which over time has only been strengthened with each challenge from apparent exceptions (Harcourt 1996).

---

[8] Some 25 species of Old World monkeys and apes exhibit conspicuous sexual swellings at mid-cycle, and, as was pointed out years ago by Clutton-Brock and Harvey (1976), most of these breed in multi-male systems. Exceptions to this generalization include the West African drill, three species whose breeding systems are not yet known, and *Papio hamadryas*, which although living today in unimale breeding systems, only recently diverged from multi-male ancestors. (For list see Hrdy, 1988; Table 6.2.)

Prehominid origins of patriarchy

At first glance, the extremely large testes of supposedly monogamous tamarins failed to conform to the model. However, subsequent field studies revealed that tamarins in fact often breed in polyandrous arrangements. Similarly, gibbons who have long been held up as paragons of primate monogamy exhibited slightly larger than expected testes and modest (and I wonder if these are not facultatively expressed?) sexual swellings. Gibbons too were considered a challenge to sexual selection theories (Dahl and Nadler 1992), until reports appeared of extra-pair copulations and mate swapping among socially, but not necessarily reproductively, monogamous lesser apes (Palombit 1992). Such findings transformed larger than anticipated testes in tamarins and gibbons into a validated *prediction of*, rather than challenge to, the model.

So why should females ever mate with more than one male? A variety of benefits have been postulated, some genetic in nature, others having to do with non-genetic processes (see Table 6.2).

To date, there is no evidence from non-human primates to indicate that females select males on the basis of specific genetic attributes, data on a par with Petrie's (1994) discovery of increased fitness for peafowl who chose peacock's with many-eyed tails, or data beginning to emerge for humans (Thornhill and Gangestad 1996). Thus, even those who (like myself) emphasise female agency are for the time being (until more genetic information is available) compelled to remain agnostic concerning whether or not non-human primate females choose mates on the basis of genes (Small 1993; Manson 1995; Bercovitch 1995).

As DNA paternity data begins to emerge for macaques and baboons, there are no obvious winners able to monopolize paternity. In general, various males who achieve high rank (but not necessarily the top rank) gain roughly in proportion to how long they manage to stay alive and in the troop (de Ruiter *et al.* 1992; Keane *et al.* 1977; and especially Altmann *et al.* 1996). These findings are consistent with the idea that rank matters but that it is also hard for any one male to monopolize ovulating females. It is not clear what it says about female choice, since as William Hamilton has pointed out, an absence of obvious manoeuvres on the part of females may simply indicate that females do not seek to circumvent a system biased in favour of high-ranking, long-lasting males (pers. comm. 4 December 1995).

However, it would not be advisable to extrapolate from these cercopithecine cases to all primates so early in the game. Field observations for supposedly monogamous titi monkeys and gibbons, as well as one-male groups of langurs indicate that under some circumstances females are *not* statisfied with the status quo, and leave their group to solicit outsiders as well as dominant resident males. Among langur monkeys at Mount Abu, for example, the average duration of male residence in a troop of breeding females was twenty-seven months. Females exhibited the highest rate of 'adulterous' solicitations of males outside the troop in the case of a troop where the dominant male had been there over five years, long enough for him to mate with his four-year-old daughters from his first year in residence (Hrdy 1977; 137–41, esp. table 5.6).

Results from paternity data on wild chimpanzees in the Tai forest in West Africa offer even stronger evidence that females sometimes insist on casting their net wider to include males outside their current community. Seven of thirteen infants who survived to provide DNA samples (collected from hair) were sired by males *outside* the local community (Gagneux *et al.* 1997). These females were casting their nets very wide indeed. But why? Were there demographic circumstances at Tai that made (normally mobile) chimpanzee females particularly eager to solicit outsiders, or environmental variables that reduced the costs to a female of leaving her community for a 24-hour period? Was there a general inclination to solicit multiple, outside males? Or were females attracted by specific attributes in males there?

Reduced importance of female choice for genes is implied

but scarcely demonstrated by the nature of primate sexual dimorphism. Accoutrements of male–male competition, like larger body size and canine teeth, are more salient than ornamental traits like peacock's tail, though there are some obvious exceptions: facial coloration of male mandrills; gibbon songs; human beards; the male anogenital colorations Darwin had noted in 1876.

The existence of a correlation between number of females and duration of average intervals between births (reported for *Macaca fascicularis* and *Presbytis entellus*) has led some authors to propose that sperm may be a limiting resource, and even to suggest that females solicit multiple males *in order to* deplete sperm available to other females (Small 1988; Sommer 1989). But it seems circular to argue that females solicit multiple partners in order to overcome sperm depletion caused by multiple matings. Even less convincing (as an ultimate explanation) is the argument that assertive female sexuality evolved *in order to generate competition at the level of the sperm*. Unquestionably, there has been selection on male primates to compete at the level of sperm resulting in large testes and voluminous ejaculate, and possibly even specialized sperm, and females have had to make the best of this.

Baker and Bellis (1995) discuss sperm competition in primates generally, and humans in particular. In contrast to Harcourt (1996) who argues that 'The human datum falls just below the testes weight/body weight regression line, as expected from the rarity with which most human females mate with more than one male around the time of ovulation', Baker and Bellis suggest that female-solicited extra-pair copulations around ovulation are sufficiently common to maintain selection at the level of sperm *in modern humans*. Although Baker and Bellis for various reasons (including the use of self-selected samples for their survey) may overemphasize the role of female infidelity while perhaps underemphasizing male coercion, there clearly do exist *some subpopulations* where the conditions for their sperm

competition model are met for humans. Furthermore, primatologists are going to need to do some rethinking regarding
genera such as *Hylobates*, previously presumed to be uni-
male and that clearly fall beneath Harcourt's regression line,
for we now recognize that they are not strictly monogamous
(Palombit 1992).

Data points that fall near Harcourt's regression line (as the
human datum point does) will almost certainly include
species where philandering is an important component of
breeding systems, compared to genera that are both socially
and reproductively monogamous (like *Aotus*). Even if there
is not currently enough sperm competition in humans to
jump-start evolution of the different morphs of sperm or
modes of selective sperm rejection and selection that Baker
and Bellis hypothesize, I believe we have to take seriously the
possibility raised by Robert Smith (1994) and Baker and
Bellis (1995) that sperm competition has played a role in
human evolution, and that under particular breeding systems
involving low levels of a paternal investment, sperm competition continues to be important. From a female's perspective,
however, such sperm competition is more probably an unfortunate consequence of polyandrous matings than something
females were selected to promote. Competition inside her
reproductive tract is, from a female's perspective, scarcely the
optimal arena for male–male competition to take place, even
though once such competition gets going in males, females
may have no choice but to make the best of it.

A female primate's highest initial priorities should involve
survival of the daughters and sons she produces. Rewards to
be gained from conceiving a son who himself produces competitive sperm can only be reaped if that 'sexy son' survives
to maturity and also happens to compete successfully for
opportunities to mate; companion benefits will be completely
lost on daughters unless they survive to produce successful
sons. To the extent that genes affect offspring quality, females
should fare better under a 'priority of access' system (distinguishing between individual males) than under a system

emphasizing priority of fertilization (distinguishing between sperm).

And what about the nongenetic rationales? At the non-genetic level, there has been little progress using primate data to test the various hypotheses. Two earlier hypotheses, the 'prostitution hypothesis' (Zuckerman 1932; Symons 1979), suggeting that females trade sex for favours (e.g. access to male-controlled food resources, like meat) and Sherfey's idea (1966) that copulations leading to orgasm have therapeutic benefits for females, are still subscribed to in some circles (the idea dates back to Greek Hippocratic authors like Galen, and is also assumed by various tribal peoples such as the !Kung San (Shostak 1981: 287). The hypothesis that females might influence the survival of their offspring by manipulating information available to males about paternity (suggested by Hrdy for langurs in 1974, and extended to other primates in 1979) has been tested, but alas the predictions that it generates have been substantiated among birds (Burke *et al.* 1989; Davies 1992), not among the primates for whom the hypothesis was first proposed.

Female dunnocks (*Prunella modularis*) solicit multiple males who in turn help to feed and care for chicks more or less in proportion to their sexual access to the mother when she was fertile (Davies 1992). That is, both the 'alpha' *and* the 'beta' male were significantly more likely to feed the young if they had fathered, or even if they could have fathered, the young. Consistent with the paternity confusion hypothesis, DNA fingerprinting revealed that males were often, *but not always*, accurate in their paternity 'assessments'. Furthermore, beta males who failed to mate were most likely to harass incubating females, and may even be responsible for destroying eggs.

Tantalizing, in the light of Davies' findings on dunnocks, is the case of the related species, *Prunella collaris*. These Japanese accentors live in multi-male, multi-female groups, rather like baboons or chimps. Masahiko Nakamura (1990) notes that 'the female's cloacal region protrudes and turns scarlet' during periods of fertility, making these birds the only case of conspicuously advertised sexual swellings outside of the Order Primates that I know of.

Nakamura hypothesizes that the swellings evolved to promote sperm competition. Yet swellings evolved among females, and (as will be discussed) females have nothing to gain from shifting the arena of male–male competition to competition between sperm. I suggest that the evolutionary sequence went: female accentors were selected to mate with multiple males for their own reasons (perhaps to confuse paternity), rendering 'sexual swellings' advantageous and leading to competition at the level of sperm.

The hypothesis that a female might inhibit males from subsequently attacking her infant, or else elicit extra protection or support for her offspring by casting wide the net of possible paternity, predicts that past consortships do indeed affect male behaviour towards the offspring of former consorts (Hrdy 1974, 1979). Observations in support of this hypothesis remain roughly the same as those that inspired it to begin with: (1) in species like savanna baboons, barbary macaques, and humans *possible progenitors and former consorts of the mother look out for the well-being of infants* (Taub 1980; Altmann *et al.* 1980); and (2) in a wide array of animals, including some sixteen species of Old and New World monkeys and Great Apes, *infanticide by adult males—which can be a major source of infant mortality—is most likely to occur when males enter a group from outside it, or else suddenly rise from a subordinate non-breeding to a breeding position within the group* (Hausfater and Hrdy 1984; Daly and Wilson 1988; Parmigiani and vom Saal 1994); but see also Sussman *et al.* 1995 for dissenting opinions, and reply by Hrdy *et al.* 1995). Infanticide by adult males has been reported for more than a dozen species of anthropoid primates, and preliminary information is also beginning to emerge for infanticide among several species of prosimians (Wright 1995; Pereira and Weiss 1991).

Prehominid origins of patriarchy

Based on data from the longest running relevant field study, spanning sixteen years of observation by over a dozen researchers of a population of Hanuman langurs at Jodhpur, Rajasthan, India, Volker Sommer calculates that of 112 infants present in troops when new males forcibly ousted the former resident male, 82 per cent were attacked by the new males, though not all were killed. Infant mortality due to infanticide was estimated to be 33 per cent of live births. In 96 per cent of the Jodhpur infanticides discussed above, the infanticidal male subsequently gained sexual access to the mother, although in at least 40 per cent of those cases, he had to share that access with other males (Sommer 1994). Apparently, gaining exclusive access to females was beyond the capacity even of males who succeeded in usurping rival males as resident male in a breeding troop.

Infanticide is a protean phenomenon across animals, perhaps especially so in humans. Cases superficially similar to the langur case are reported anecdotally in societies with long traditions of raiding for women (e.g. biblical accounts; women kidnapped among the Yanamamo where suckling infants may be killed outright, or left behind, with the same physiological outcomes: death for the infant, earlier resumption of ovulatory cycles for the mother). However, most documented cases of infanticide among humans involve one or more parents, or else substitute parents residing in the same household. Currently, researchers like Martin Daly and Margo Wilson tend to attribute the elevated risk of infants with unrelated males associated with their mothers, now well documented in Western societies, to 'discriminative parental solicitude'. Adults caring for infants may have a higher threshold for responding with solicitude towards offspring that are unrelated, poorly timed, or otherwise poor bets for transforming parental investment into successful breeding adults (Hrdy 1992; Daly and Wilson 1988).

It has been argued that this casting of the net wide so as to elicit protection or resources from several *possible* fathers can only backfire, since males less than certain of paternity will never invest (e.g. Symons 1982: 182). But there is now a great deal of evidence for various primates—especially baboons and humans—that so long as male care is neither exclusive nor tremendously costly, males routinely 'err' on the conservative side of the margin of error surrounding paternity. They look out for and preferentially provision the offspring of former mates, offspring that might possibly be, but are not definitely, their own (Altmann 1980; Hrdy 1986; for updates of the nonhuman primate record and for ethnographic cases that I have only recently become aware of, see Hrdy 1999: 214–219; 245–51).

Social theorists and literary figures concerned with human nature, encompassing a wide range of male-oriented perspectives–Samuel Johnson, Jean Jacques Rousseau, Friedrich Engels, August Strindberg—have remarked on their sex's sensitivity concerning uncertain paternity and its implications. But paternity uncertainty has rarely been a topic of empirical study. In one of the few empirical case studies among tribal peoples, behavioural ecologists Kim Hill and Hilyard Kaplan reported that women among Ache foragers in eastern Paraguay routinely rely on former consorts to increase protection and resources available to their offspring. Interviews with seventeen women reveal that each of sixty-six offspring was attributed to a mean number of 2.1 possible progenitors. This phenomenon is sufficiently pervasive that the Ache recognize different categories of fatherhood. 'One type refers to the man who is married to a woman when her child is born. Another type refers to the man or men with whom she has had extramarital relations just prior to or during her pregnancy. The third type refers to the man who *she* believes actually inseminated her . . .' (Hill and Kaplan 1988: 289). The presence of such 'godfathers' means more game brought in (meat comprises 60 per cent of Ache diets). Marjorie Shostak (1981: 281) provides similar examples of lovers who provide their paramours with supplementary food among San foraging people in the Kalahari desert.

Possible fathers also provide critical protection for immatures against other men. Infanticide/pedicide rates among the Ache are high, with 12 per cent of liveborn children between the ages of birth and five years dying as a consequence. Data on twenty-six cases of child homicide are reported by Hill and Hurtado (1996). Loss of male protectors renders children particularly vulnerable, and they may be killed either by other band members who no longer wish to provide for them or by the mother's subsequent husband. Hill and Kaplan report that children whose reported biological father dies before the children reach the age of fifteen are significantly more likely to die. Of children whose fathers died, 43 per cent of a sample of sixty-seven died prior to age fifteen, compared to 19.3 per cent of 171 children whose fathers remained alive until after the child reached age fifteen (Hill and Kaplan, 1988: 298; and Hill and Hurtado 1996 for an in-depth discussion of Ache life histories).

There are also some anatomical reasons for suspecting that female primates may have been selected to mate with a range of male partners. Orgasmic 'reward' systems dependent on prolonged stimulation of the female genitalia—now documented among rhesus and stump-tailed macaques (Burton 1970; Goldfoot *et al.* 1980; Slob *et al.* 1986, 1991)—can be viewed as having evolved in non-human primate females to condition them to continue soliciting sequential partners. Although Symons (1979) and Gould (1995) have insisted that female orgasms, and the clitoris (an organ whose only known function is to translate physical stimulation into psycho-physiological sensations sometimes associated with orgasm) are incidental, present in females because they are selected for in males, this conclusion ignores comparative evidence for different primate species.[9]

[9] For further discussion and references see Hrdy 1988: esp. 122–5, 131, n. 42. Gould (1995), in an essay entitled 'Male Nipples and Clitoral Ripples' critiques the 'adaptationist assumption that orgasm must have evolved for Darwinian utility in promoting reproductive success'. In doing so, he cites me selectively and out of context, providing no reference which would permit readers to put my views in context. In fact, the comments Dr Gould cites appeared in Hrdy (1981: 165–72), and followed a long discussion of the undue readiness scientists

Primate clitorises vary in size, shape, and placement between species in ways that are sometimes parallel (or 'homologous') with the size and shape of the penis, and sometimes not. For example, the clitoris is relatively and absolutely larger in both species of chimpanzee than it is in humans, while the penis is relatively and absolutely larger in humans than in either species of chimpanzee (McFarland 1976; Baker and Bellis 1995: 167–71). Even in the relatively brief evolutionary time-span since *Pan paniscus* diverged from other chimpanzees, there has been sufficient selection pressure for substantial changes in the bonobo clitoris to evolve (presumably due to the significance in bonobo mating systems of frontal rubbing of the genitals during sexual behaviour). In addition to heterosexual couplings, Amy Parish has recently argued that sexual behaviour between two females plays a role in forging social alliances between unrelated females, counteracting negative effects for females constrained to live in patrilocal communities, without female kin (Parish and de Waal 1992; Parish 1994, 1996).

Whatever the explanation for observed hypersexuality in this species turns out to be, the bonobo clitoris is distinctively shaped and frontally placed (Dahl 1985); I am not aware of any corresponding (or 'homologous') difference in the bonobo penis (Short 1979; Parish pers. comm.). Unless one wishes to argue that the female bonobo's remarkable morphology (already apparent in young females) has resulted ontogenetically from bonobo sexual practices (frontal genital–genital

have of assuming that selection weighs primarily on males. I never suggested that orgasms were current adaptations (they may or may not be, see esp. Baker and Bellis 1995, who argue that they are). Rather, I proposed that orgasmic rewards systems were selected for in prehominid contexts, and are a contemporary vestige of past selection pressures. This hypothesis, explaining original selection pressures for orgasmic responses in females, is silent concerning current function; it neither presupposes, nor rules out, the possibility that orgasms which evolved in a different context, have subsequently become enlisted in maintaining contemporary pair bonds, or even, as Baker and Bellis argue, enlisted in discriminating preferred from non-preferred sperm. Whatever the result, no one should be surprised by the imperfections of such a system, the product of a long, opportunistic, and makeshift evolutionary history.

rubbing during infancy), it seems likely that selection has operated on bonobos to favour the different shape and placement
of the clitoris in *paniscus* compared to *troglodytes*.

Facultative expression of different patterns of sexual activity in *paniscus* and *troglodytes* may in fact have provided precursors or 'pre-adaptations' for eventual speciation in these
Great Apes (e.g. see discussions of flexible phenotypes in
West-Eberhard 1991, 1992). As West-Eberhard suggests:
'Perhaps the best way to begin to shake off the inhibitions
that come from an obsession with stability, equilibrium and
stasis, and constraints is to think about . . . sexual behavior'
(West-Eberhard 1992: 60).

Flexible phenotypes in coercive social systems

'Concealed ovulation' (or, more nearly, 'absence of advertised oestrus'), 'continuous (situation-dependent) receptivity', face-to-face copulations, and a female capacity for
orgasm which have long been considered uniquely human
attributes that evolved to cement pair bonds (Morris 1967;
Lovejoy 1981), are viewed here as part of a much older prehominid heritage that does not assume monogamous mating
systems (Hrdy 1981; Sillen-Tullberg and Moller 1993). This
would have been the 'raw material' available to our ancestors in forging variably monogamous-to-polygynous, uni-
male mating systems and developing diverse systems of
marriage and inheritance that define modern *Homo sapiens*.

Understanding exactly how the sexual discretion that so
struck Darwin came to characterize so many women (compared to, say, bonobos) will require a combination of evolutionary, historical, and developmental approaches. Although
it may seem circuitous for those whose primary interest is
humans to focus so much on female libido in non-human primates (e.g. Rossi 1995), I am convinced that a broad comparative perspective can, as in this instance, lead to new, and
potentially very illuminating questions: why do women differ

from other female primates in respect to sexual discretion or 'coyness'?

Clearly, female primates are more sexually assertive than Darwin and his successors realized and by extension, so were our remote ancestresses. It is not true that ancestral humans 'were faced with a unique paternity problem not faced by other primate males,' nor that humans are the only species in which males have a problem being certain of paternity. Yet the idea persists that 'cryptic ovulation' is uniquely human, and that 'In contrast to human males (a non-human primate male) can be fairly confident of his paternity . . .' (Buss 1994a: 66).

As a consequence of such oversights, there was a second miscalculation. We underestimated the full extent and importance of repressive strategies by males—some evolved, some possibly learned (Kummer *et al.* 1974)—in order to counter such sexuality, subverting female mate choices by harassing, sequestering, punishing, or intimidating them, and by monopolizing access to the resources that females need to breed. Although feminists and animal behaviourists have in fact long understood that coercion of females played some role, and certainly sociobiologists were aware of forcible subversion of female choice, with a few exceptions, subversion of female choice has not been a focus for study until recently.

When a male langur enters a breeding system from outside it and kills infants sired by his predecessor, he usurps female 'choice' in the sense that he eliminates the genes of the last male she mated with. At the same time, he also presents her with an offer that she cannot refuse except at great reproductive cost to herself: if she boycotts the male who killed her infant, delay in her subsequent conception will put her at a reproductive disadvantage in competition with other females for genetic representation in the next generation. Thus does the infanticidal male also subvert the mother's *choice* of the timing of reproduction.

Rather than bear the evolutionary costs of a barren interlude, infanticide puts the female (now freed from lactational amenorrhea) under pressure to conceive again after a shorter interbirth interval than might otherwise be optimal for her (Hrdy 1974, 1979; Leland *et al.* 1984; Sommer 1994), imposing a degree of physiological stress that (if reproduction costs wild monkeys as much as most now assume it does) detracts from her survival and long-term reproductive success.

Viewed from a female perspective, male coercion takes on a different meaning from that animal behaviorists typically assign to a topic like 'male dominance'. This new meaning is being explored by Gowaty (1997, 1998), Tim Clutton-Brock, and Parker (1995*a*,*b*), and Smuts and Smuts (1993).

In recognition of the costs imposed on females by such interference, some animal behaviourists, and evolutionary theorists have proposed giving 'sexual coercion' pride of place—or at least third place—in Darwinian sexual selection theory (Smuts 1992; Smuts and Smuts 1993), essentially turning 'sexual selection' from a two-part to a tripartite theory: (1) *male–male competition*; (2) *female choice*; and (3) *female coercion by males*. Episodes of male coercion of females can be located in the animal behaviour literature from Darwin onwards, and since Trivers (1972), sociobiologists have tended to view conflicting interests of males and females as a routine by-product of sexual selection. However, the theoretical significance of 'male coercion' of females, as well as the circumstances where it was likely to be important (e.g. in non-territorial, polygynous species like hamadryas baboons) was first emphasized by Searcy and Yasukawa (1989).

Subsequently, data on reproductive costs imposed on females bound in polygynous marriages among Australian aborigines were also deemed consistent with the 'male coercion model' (Chisholm and Burbank 1991), the first human application of the model. More importantly, Chisholm and Burbank called attention to the possibility of men and women negotiating 'compromises' of their conflicting interests. For example, although women who remain as their husband's only wife are better off in terms of fitness than women who have to share resources with co-wives, sororally polygynous arrangements (where co-wives are sisters) are potentially far more cooperative and less disadvantageous than when co-wives are unrelated.

A key point to emerge from this evolutionary consciousness-raising is that once females are viewed as active agents, we are forced to look harder at male subversion of female choice as well as identifying female strategies to counter and ameliorate such male counter-strategies (Hrdy 1977), groping to identify and measure processes in what Gowaty (1997) has termed the endless and ongoing 'dialectics of sex' (1997). If some of the domination males used in the course of competing seems unnecessarily violent or 'gratuitous'—occasionally, a female is injured or killed—such force is nonetheless viewed as, on average, an effective way of guaranteeing female compliance (Smuts 1992; Clutton-Brock and Parker 1995*a*).

Departing from feminist analyses, evolutionists are not convinced that males subvert female choices simply for the satisfaction of doing so, or to show off to others that they can. Rather, they assume that males do so because on average such tactics make them reproductively more competitive with other males.

An important concept, male coercion. But to recognize it do we actually need to revamp Darwin's theory of sexual selection theory? Clearly, both components (male–male competition and female choice) are more complicated than Darwin—with his focus on competing males and coy females—originally contemplated. Nevertheless, Darwin's focus on intrasexual competition remains a brilliantly serviceable framework (apologies to those who wish it were not so, or think that competition must be a projection of my capitalist imagination).

Rather than tinker with the armature, it makes more sense to retain Darwin's overarching assumption that when males compete, *the nature of the ultimate goal is to reproductively out-compete other members of the same sex*, and then go on to enquire further about specific ecological, developmental, and historical processes that shaped motivations and behaviors that nevertheless originally evolved in the service of male–male competition. For, as Mary Jane West-Eberhard points out, without intrasexual selection (usually meaning male–male competition) there would be no point to female choice or to male attempts to 'bypass female choice and "coyness" by force . . .' (West-Eberhard 1991).

There are many permutations of sexual selection. The fallout from male–male competition and female counter-strategies to male coercion can take multiple forms (e.g. males can compete by trying to exclude rival males from contact with fertile females, or can tolerate contact but compete at the level of the sperm as Parker pointed out years ago, etc.). Indeed in the human case, were it not for the extraordinary mobility and ease of interbreeding in our species, I think it possible that our facultative sexual natures combined with variable behavioural ecologies, mores, and institutional histories would have long ago led to subspecies as different in sexual habits and attributes as *Pan troglodytes* and *Pan paniscus*!

Male–male reproductive competition among anthropoid primates takes place against a backdrop of female sexual assertiveness. Just as male coercion is a problem primate females must cope with, females soliciting multiple partners or wandering away from their 'breeding group' is the problem from a resident male's perspective. Whether sexual swellings and situation-dependent receptivity evolved as female counter-strategies to forestall infanticide, and to secure male protection and assistance, or for some other reason, the fact remains that none of these behaviours evolved in a vacuum.

Selection on males to counter female strategies would in turn have operated to select (in the multi-male breeders) for larger testes and more competitive sperm, thereby moving competition over 'promiscuous' females to another zone.

Alternatively, males in uni-male systems like open habitat desert-dwelling hamadryas baboons, or gorillas living in deep forests, would be forced to devote energy to excluding other males and/or sequestering females rather than producing more and more competitive sperm (Harcourt 1996). The more innovative apes, like *Homo sapiens*, invented whole new modes of policing females involving claustration, indoctrination, and surveillance (Dickemann 1979, 1981).

Understanding the unique role that sexual 'coyness' (modesty, prudence, or attention to 'reputation' might be better terms) still plays in our own species will demand economic, cultural, developmental, and historic, as well as evolutionary, perspectives. What has happened in the course of hominid evolution *and history* to alter selection for assertive female sexuality? Relative sexual freedom is permitted women under some circumstances, but the vast majority of human cultures practise a double standard of sexual morality (Broude and Greene 1976; Broude 1980), which combined with the human capacity for language and propensity for gossip, subjects any woman who cannot account for her whereabouts to damaging, even lethal, penalties, as well as to internally produced feelings of mortification and shame.

Given the long time-frame for the development of such traits as male sexual jealousy, female 'coyness', modesty or discretion, it is worthwhile taking seriously the proposition that such emotions may be more than cultural constructions, as in the case of blushing (e.g. see Darwin's 1872 chapter on 'Self-attention, Shame, Shyness, Modesty, Blushing'). More importantly, we need to be careful not to mistake for supposed 'species-typical' universal traits (male preferences for neotenous females, female preferences for rich men) which may in fact be ontogenetic coping strategies in a socially constraining world.

The elaborate subversion of female counter-strategies is, as Dickemann points out, ultimately just another form of male–male competition in Darwin's classical sense. Even when accomplished by prevailing over and controlling females and by tapping into internally produced constraints on females to breed again sooner rather than boycott aggressive males, the male's evolutionary 'goal' is the same, outproducing rival males.

The fact that ultimately selection pressures are on males relative to other males, rather than on males in relation to what they do to females, does not alter the consequences for females, or make them any less detrimental. Obviously, curtailing female freedom of movement interferes with her foraging, or (in humans) other modes of production. Sequestered grouping may increase female–female competition or subject her to unhealthy living conditions (more crowded, exposed to pathogens, etc.). (Note that we could also turn victimization around, and lament the reproductive losses imposed on asymmetrical males by female choices, or on domineering males by female peregrinations.)

Less obviously, we could consider the ways that sperm competition is probably detrimental for females. Even if it is true that 'sexy sons' inherit their father's attributes in this respect, any pay-off from producing competitive sperm would not arise until after a son had survived long enough to mature and become competitive for mates.

Given that the most viable or mobile sperm does not necessarily transport genes that code for superior phenotypes in terms of infant survival, or whatever most matters in the mother's current environment, or that fathers who produce competitive sperm need not necessarily create advantageous conditions for infant survival, in species like primates where individuals are only long-lived *if* they survive the very vulnerable infant and juvenile years, and only reproductively successful if they are long-lived, I would expect competitive sperm to fall rather far down the 'list' of a mother's criteria for an ideal mate. It is already apparent that ejaculate quality need not correlate with other measures of survivorship or phenotypic success (Birkhead *et al.* 1995).

Among humans, the most important male strategies

involve not just physical coercion, intimidation and indoctrination of females, but monopolization by patrilines of resources needed to survive and successfully rear offspring, forcing females (and their families) to favour wealthy mates, and further encouraging the parents of sons to channel resources in ways that make their children competitive (Dickemann 1979; Boone 1986).

Such circumstances encourage the development of complex marriage and intergenerational systems that concentrate resources in male hands (Hartung 1976; Voland 1984; Boone 1986; Borgerhoff-Mulder 1988; Sieff 1990; Betzig 1992; Hrdy and Judge 1993). Although cultural anthropologists and historians will no doubt find such interpretations overly reductionist, the focus on male–male competition in Darwin's original theory of sexual selection clarifies the motivations underlying manifold and very diverse processes contributing to male domination.

To sum up then, feminists have argued that patriarchy is a cultural and historical creation by men and women in a process that took some 2,500 years. By contrast, a Darwinian perspective—without necessarily discounting historical processes involved—would lead us to push the search for patriarchy's origins back millions of years earlier by asking the additional question of why so many hominid males and their patrilines have experienced such an urgent need to control females?

Male resource control constrains female choices

> Men argued with the giants that precede them; women argued against the oppressive weight of millennia of patriarchal thought . . .
>
> Gerda Lerner, 1993

When male dominance comes bolstered by patrilocal living arrangements (males not only physically stronger but advantaged by the availability of relatives, e.g. Quinn 1977) sons will have greater resource-holding potential than daughters, encouraging parents to further bias intergenerational transfers of resources in favour of sons who can keep hold of cattle or land, versus daughters who are particularly vulnerable from having it taken away or diverted to their husband's lineage.

Across all well-studied species of primates, humans provide the only well-documented cases of female choice for male attributes.[10] These cases involve women's choice of wealthy husbands (Borgerhoff-Mulder 1990; Buss 1994*a, b*). But practically speaking, a woman's preference for a wealthy man can be attributed to the fact that males monopolize ownership of productive resources (cattle, land, high-paying jobs). A women gains access to the resources she needs to survive and reproduce through her mate. Unfortunately, such arguments might be taken to mean that if patriarchy has evolutionary roots, it must be inevitable. This is not so. Many biologically based predispositions are extremely malleable (Hrdy 1990; Gowaty 1995). Consider a single example.

Since the dawn of civilization (Lerner 1986) and probably far longer (Ghiglieri 1987; Rodseth *et al.* 1991; Murdock 1976) many different systems of intergenerational transfer from parents to offspring of territories and/or resources have developed with a common feature of favouring males. Colonial America was no exception (Judge and Hrdy 1992, in prep.). Most fathers bequeathed most of their resources to one or more sons, more or less excluding daughters, who with no legal right to own property, and no powerful allies, had no way to defend property ownership. (Mothers do not even appear in these probate records until the eighteenth century; married women did not have the legal right to own property, and hence had little to bequeath).

Yet, as demographic, ecological and legal conditions changed over the course of the eighteenth and nineteenth centuries, so did parental treatment of heirs. As Debra

---

[10] Other cases I can think of are much more speculative—involving, for example, female choice of males who can defend her infants against other males, as in gorillas.

Judge (1995) has demonstrated, smaller families meant that more parents only had daughters as potential heirs. Married Women's Property Acts during the latter half of the nineteenth century meant that daughters, even those with no kin on hand, had a powerful new ally—the state, which would intervene to protect women against forcible confiscation of their property by more powerful members of society. New legal rights meant that parents with smaller families, possibly without sons to bequeath wealth to, had a novel option. Inheritance by daughters increased dramatically.

New property rights were critical to the experiment in equal rights and increasingly equal opportunities women in Western societies are currently engaged in. Age-old tendencies biased parental preferences; preferential treatment of sons is a very ancient and a very widespread hominoid pattern. Many factors reinforce its persistence however, son preferences is *not* inevitable given social or ecological changes that alter cost–benefit ratios to parents (Hrdy 1990; Smuts 1992).

Hence, when some evolutionary psychologists and their popularizers propose—under the guise of feminist sensibility and progressive thinking—that women would benefit from polygynous marriages, because polygyny while harming subelite men (forced to go wifeless), *benefits* women, we need to be clear that patriarchal property arrangements are *taken for granted*. In this imagined polygynous-feminist utopia— several women would be permitted to share access to wealthy men instead of being forced to settle for some economically inadequate also-ran or worse, a non-provider (Wright 1994: 98–101). But note that the system proposed remains a patriarchal one where male patrilines still control access to productive resources (and/or higher-paying jobs).

Like traditional sociobiologists, these evolutionary psychologists also invoke sexual selection theory to explain patriarchal attributes. But the argument is fundamentally different. Buss, for example, hypothesizes that *female preferences* selected for male acquisitiveness and a high motivation to compete for resources. As Buss (1996: 307–8) puts it:

Women's preferences ... established an important set of ground rules for men in their competition with one another. Based on sexual selection theory, the desires of one sex establish the critical dimensions along which members of the opposite sex compete. Since ancestral men tended to place a premium on women's physical appearance ... this established attractiveness as a major dimension along which women compete with one another ... Analogously, women's desires for men with resources established the acquisition of resources as a major dimension of men's competition with each other.

Hence, even mens' 'larger bodies and more powerful status drives' are attributed to 'women's mating preferences' for men with resources (Buss 1994a: 47).

By contrast, behavioural ecologists and sociobiologists (Hrdy 1981; Emlen 1995; Hrdy and Judge 1993) tend to give more weight to comparative evidence across taxa, variation within species, and paleontological evidence for hominids and other primates through time. Sexual dimorphism correlates with degree of polygyny, but there are no known correlations with male control of resources. Indeed, compared to other pongids, Australopithecines, and earlier hominids, modern humans are *less* dimorphic than one would expect of an ape of our size; this is the opposite of what we would expect if female choice for males able to control resources had anything to do with male body size. Monopolization of resources is greater now than at any previous point in hominid history, yet modern *Homo sapiens* falls among the least dimorphic apes (McHenry 1996 and many others). Clearly, sexual dimorphism, as well as male control of resources, *preceded* female choice for males with resources. For example, Hrdy and Judge (1993) point to male philopatry, availability to sons of patrilineal allies, preferential treatment of sons by parents, and male-biased transmission of territorial control and of resources as prior to, and setting the

erences for resource-controlling mates by both
10 migrate from outside to join mates) and by
. Furthermore, male philopatry predisposing
m coalitions with patrilineal male relatives
irces male dominance over females (Hrdy 1981;
). In such systems, behavioural ecologists
would expect that females will choose males on the basis
of resources, and this prediction is supported by a growing
body of empirical evidence (Borgerhoff-Mulder 1987, 1990;
Buss 1991). But empirical support for this prediction does
not mean that female choice for males *was responsible* for
males being competitive or for males controlling resources
in the first place. Both male–male competition for females
and male control of productive resources were already present in the hominid line, and preceded the development of
female preferences for resource-holding males in the human
case.

For women (and their offspring) not only depend on husbands to protect and provide for them, but as is typical in
patriarchal societies, a woman's status is defined by whether
or not, and whom, she marries. Only as this situation changes,
would criteria for mate choice gradually be expected to also
change. But such an experiment in unconstrained choice,
what Gowaty (pers. comm.) terms 'free female choice' has
not yet been tried on any large scale or over any period of
time. Furthermore, it remains unknown what 'free' choice for
anyone committed to reproduction even looks like. Without
the relevant experiments or comparative studies, we can not
claim to know yet what the innate or 'universal' female mate
choice criteria are, although we can be reasonably confident
that male control of resources was *not* brought about by
a 'universal' psychological preference among women for
wealthy men. The 'patriarchal constraints' hypothesis is silent
as to whether female preferences for resource-rich males are
innate 'human universals' or primarily learned in the course
of socialization.

Whether learned or evolved, however, the 'patriarchal constraints hypothesis' predicts that when female status and access to resources are not dependent on her mate's status, a female will use a range of criteria, not primarily prestige and wealth, for mate selection. Furthermore, when resources are important for reproduction, and when females possess (or are able to obtain) resources, males will be likely to value resource potential (good territories, maternal fat stores, whatever) along with or over 'beauty'. Given the same playing field, and controlling for body strength (which indeed is rendered feasible by modern technologies and current legal protections), men and women are predicted to be comparably motivated when competing for those resources that pertain to their long-term reproductive success even though the form that competition takes may differ (Hrdy 1981: 129–30). These ideas have important implications for contemporary debates.

Some critics of affirmative action find in evolutionary psychology support for their opposition. They argue that males are by nature more aggressive, assertive, competitive and achievement motivated than females are (Browne 1995, esp. 1017ff.). The 'glass ceiling' on remuneration for women versus men in our own society is then attributed to innately less competitive temperaments in women (Browne 1995) rather than to male-biased institutions and the quite different fitness trade-offs in the case of men versus women, since for women single-minded pursuit of high-status jobs has typically meant choosing between investing in a career and investing in offspring; men have had more leeway in finding women to invest for them.

Ignored in these analyses is the fact that in other species of primates, females do compete directly for the resources they need to survive, to reproduce, and to rear surviving offspring (Hrdy 1981). To the extent that humans are exceptional in this respect, to the extent that women differ from other primates by competing for resources indirectly, competing for resources by competing for mates who provide them, we must ask, why?

Sarah Blaffer Hrdy

Replying to Spencer

'Did you ever hear the like on't' said Mr. Tulliver, as Maggie retired. 'It's a pity but what she'd been the lad . . . as I picked the mother because she wasn't o'er 'cute—bein' a good-looking woman too . . . but I picked her from her sisters o' purpose 'cause she was a bit weak, like . . . But you see when a man's got brains himself, there's no knowing where they'll run to ; an' a pleasant sort o' soft woman may go on breeding you stupid lads and 'cute wenches till it's like as if the world was turned topsy-turvy. It's an uncommon puzzling thing'.   (George Eliot, *Mill on the Floss*, 1860)

Ironically, one of the first Darwinian feminists to seek to destabilize Spencerian dichotomies, turning his predictable sexually selected world 'topsy-turvy', as well as to concern herself with undermining patriarchal property arrangements and to propose (by creating fictional role models) that we move away from stereotypes of non-nurturing males and nurturing but less-than-rational females (and also to suggest that we rethink the role beauty plays in evaluating female worth!) was none other than George Eliot.

Eliot was also the first Darwinian feminist to caution fellow evolutionists to pay attention to historical contingencies, individual differences, emergent properties, and to be mindful of development. I cede the last word in this Spencer essay to her.

In a letter written in December 1859 Eliot wrote to women's rights supporter and co-founder of Girton College, Barbara Bodichon, the following

We have been reading Darwin's book on the 'Origin of Species' just now . . . the book is ill-written and sadly wanting in illustrative facts—of which he has collected a vast number, but reserves there for a future book of which this smaller one is the avant-courier . . . but it will have great effect on the scientific world, causing a thorough and open discussion of a question about which people have hitherto felt timid. So the world gets on step by step towards brave clearness and honesty! But to me the Development theory [the term Eliot uses to refer to descent with modification] and all other explanations of processes by which things came to be produce a feeble impression compared with the mystery that lies under the processes. (Eliot in Haight 1954–78, Vol. 3: 224–8),

Mill on the Floss, Eliot's description of a gifted girl growing up in a male-dominated world, was written in that same year. One can read into that novel, along with *Silas Marner, Daniel Deronda*, and *Middlemarch*, carefully crafted admonitions to beware social Darwinist illusions about male and female universals. Men who imagine that they are selecting their mates on the basis of scientific principles engineered to preserve the 'welfare of the race', as did that quintessential man of science, Dr Lydgate, may rue the day. For Lydgate succumbed to the 'perfect blonde loveliness' and 'lovely little face' as neotenous 'as if she was five years old', of Rosamonde Vincy— who ruined his life. Mr Tulliver's carefully thought out intentions to marry a stupid but pretty woman also backfired when she produced handsome plodding sons and overly acute daughters.

Men (like Silas Marner) as well as women may learn to nurture, although not all women, or even all mothers (like Adam Bede's Hetty) are necessarily nurturing, and so forth. In the jargon of contemporary behavioural biology: apparently species-typical universals may merely reflect otherwise flexible phenotypes constrained by patriarchal social systems.

REFERENCES

ACTON, W. (1865). *Functions and Disorders of the Reproductive System*, (4th edn). London.

ALPER, J., J. BECKWITH, and L. G. MILLER (1978). 'Sociobiology is a Political Issue'. In *The Sociobiology Debate*, A. Caplan (ed.). New York: Harper & Row.

ALTMANN, J. *et al.* (1980). *Baboon Mothers and Infants*. Cambridge, MA: Harvard University Press.

ALTMANN, J. *et al.* (1996) 'Behavior Predicts Genetic Structure in a

Wild Primate Group'. *Proceedings of the National Academy of Sciences.*

ANDELMAN, S. (1987). 'Evolution of Concealed Ovulation in Vervet Monkeys (*Cercopithecus aethiops*)'. *American Naturalist*, **129**: 785–99.

ANDERSON, C. (1986). 'Female Age: Male Preference and Reproductive Success in Primates'. *International Journal of Primatology*, **7**: 305–26.

——and C. BIELERT (1994). 'Adolescent Exaggeration in Female Catarrhine Primates'. *Primates*, **35**: 283–300.

BAKER, R. R. and M. A. BELLIS (1995). *Human Sperm Competition: Copulation, Masturbation and Infidelity.* London: Chapman & Hall.

BATEMAN, A. J. (1948). 'Intra-sexual selection in Drosophila'. *Heredity* **26**: 349–68.

BERKOVITCH, F. (1995). 'Female Cooperation, Consortship Maintenance, and Male Mating Success in Savanna Baboons'. *Animal Behavior*, **50**: 137–49.

BETZIG, LAURA (1992). 'Roman monogamy'. *Ethology and Sociobiology*, **13**: 351–83.

BIRKHEAD, T. R., F. FLETCHER, E. J. PELLATT, and A. SAPLES (1995). 'Ejaculate Quality and the Success of Extra-pair Copulations in the Zebra Finch'. *Nature*, **337**: 442–3.

BOONE, J. (1986). 'Parental Investment and Elite Family Structure in Preindustrial States: A Case Study of Late Medieval-Early Modern Portuguese Genealogies'. *American Anthropologist*, **88**: 859–78.

BORGERHOFF-MULDER, M. (1987). 'Resources and Reproductive Success in Women, With an Example from the Kipsigis'. *Journal of Zoology.* **213**: 489–505.

——(1988). 'Reproductive Consequences of Sex-biased Inheritance for the Kipsigis'. In *Comparative Socioecology of Mammals and Man.* London: Blackwell.

——(1990). 'Kipsigis Women's Preference for Wealthy Men: Evidence for Female Choice in Mammals?' *Behavioral Ecology and Sociobiology*, **27**: 255–64.

BROUDE, G. (1980). 'Extramarital Sex Norms in Cross-cultural Perspective'. *Behavior Science Research*, **15**: 181–218.

——and S. J. GREENE (1976). 'Cross-cultural Codes on Twenty Sexual Attitudes and Practices'. *Ethology*, **15**: 410–29.

BROWNE, K. R. (1995). 'Sex and Temperament in Modern Society: A Darwinian View of the Glass Ceiling and the Gender Gap'. *Arizona Law Review*, **37**: 973–1106.

BROWNMILLER, S. (1975). *Against Our Will: Men, Women and Rape.* New York: Simon & Schuster.

BURKE, T., N. B. DAVIES, M. W. BRUFORD, and B. J. HATCHWELL (1989). 'Paternal Care and Mating Behaviour of Polyandrous Dunnocks *Prunella modularis*, Related to Paternity by DNA Fingerprinting'. *Nature*, **338**: 249–51.

BURTON, F. D. (1970). 'Sexual Climax in Female *Macaca mulatta'*. *Proc. 3rd Int. Congr. Primat., Zurich*, **3**: 180–91.

BUSS, D. (1991). 'Mate Selection for Parenting Skills (response to Chisholm)'. *Behavioral and Brain Sciences*, **14**: 520–1.

——(1994*a*). *The Evolution of Desire.* New York: Basic Books.

——(1994*b*). 'The Strategies of Human Mating'. *American Scientist*, 238–49.

——(1996). 'Sexual Conflict: Evolutionary Insight into Feminism and the "Battle of the Sexes"'. In *Sex, Power and Conflict: Evolutionary and Feminist Perspectives*, D. Buss and N. Malamuth (eds.). New York: Oxford University Press.

CHISHOLM, J. 'Whose Reproductive Value?' *Behavioral and Brain Sciences*, **14**: 519–30.

CHISHOLM, J. S. and V. BURBANK (1991). 'Monogamy and Polygyny in Southeast Arnhem Land: Male Coercion and Female Choice'. *Ethology and Sociobiology*, **12**: 291–313.

CLUTTON-BROCK, T. H. and P. HARVEY (1976). 'Evolutionary Rules and Primate Societies'. In *Growing Points in Ethology*, P. P. G. Bateson and R. A. Hinde (eds.). Cambridge, UK: Cambridge University Press.

——and G. A. PARKER (1995*a*). 'Punishment in Animal Societies'. *Nature*, **373**: 209–16.

——(1995*b*). 'Sexual Coercion in Animal Societies'. *Animal Behavior*, **49**: 1345–65.

CRONIN, H. (1991). *The Ant and the Peacock.* Cambridge, UK: Cambridge University Press.

DAHL, J. (1985). 'The External Genitalia of Female Pygmy Chimpanzees'. *Anat. Rec.* **211**: 24–8.

——and R. NADLER (1992). 'Genital Swelling in Females of the Monogamous Gibbon, *Hylobates, (H.) lar'*. *American Journal of Physical Anthropology*, **89**: 101–8.

DAHL, J. and D. G. COLLINS (1991). 'Monitoring the Ovarian Cycles of *Pan troglodytes* and *Pan paniscus*: A Comparative Approach'. *American Journal of Primatology*, **24**: 195–209.

DALY, M. and M. WILSON (1983). *Sex, Evolution and Behavior.* Boston, MA: Willard Grant Bateman Press.

——(1988). *Homicide.* New York: Aldine de Gruyter.

DARWIN, C. (1871/1974). *The Descent of Man and Selection in Relation to Sex.* Detroit MI: Gale Research Inc.

——(1872/1965). *Expressions of the Emotions in Man and Animals.* Chicago, IL: University of Chicago Press.

——(1976). 'Sexual Selection in Relation to Monkeys'. *Nature*, **15**: 18–19.

DAVIES, N. B. (1992). *Dunnock Behaviour and Social Evolution.* Oxford University Press.

DE RUITER, J. R., E. J. WICKINGS, W. SCHEFFRAHN, N. MENARD, M. BRUFORD, and M. INOUE (1992). 'Summary of Symposium on Genetic Markers from XIVth International Primatological Society Meeting, Strasbourg, August 1992'. *Primates* **43**: 469; 553–5.

DICKEMANN, M. (1979). 'The Ecology of Mating Systems in Hypergymous Dowry Societies'. *Social Science Information*, **18**: 163–95.

——(1981). 'Paternal Confidence and Dowry Competition: A Biocultural Analysis of Purdah'. In *Natural Selection and Social Behavior*, R. D. Alexander and D. Tinkle (eds.). Concord, MA: Chiron.

DIXON, A. G. (1983). 'Observations on the Evolution and Behavioral Significance of "Sexual Skin" in Female Primates'. *Advances in the Study of Behavior*, **13**: 63–106.

DOYLE, G. A. (1974). 'Behavior of Prosimians'. In *Behavior of Nonhuman Primates* (Vol. 4), A. M. Schrier and F. Stollnitz (eds.). New York: Academic Press.

DRICKAMER, L. (1974). 'A Ten-year Summary of Reproductive Data for Free-ranging *Macaca mulatta*'. *Folia Primatologica*, **21**: 61–80.

ELIOT, GEORGE (1860/1961). *Mill on the Floss.* Boston, MA: Houghton Mifflin.

EMLEN, STEVE (1995). 'An Evolutionary Theory of the Family'. *Proceedings of the National Academy of Sciences*, **92**: 8092–9.

ENGELS, F. (1884/1973). *The Origin of the Family, Private Property and the State.* New York: International Publishers.

FURUICHI, T. (1992). 'Prolonged Estrus of Females and Factors Influencing Mating in a Wild Group of Bonobos (*Pan paniscus*) in Wamba, Zaire'. In *Topics in Primatology*, Vol. 2, Behavior, Ecology and Conservation, ed. N. Itoigawa, Y. Sugiyoma G. P. Sackett, and R. K. R. Thompson. Tokyo University of Tokyo Press, 179–90.

GAGNEUX, PASCAL, DAVID S. WOODRUFF, and CHRISTOPHE BOESCH (1997). 'Furtive Mating in Female Chimpanzees'. *Nature*, **387**: 358–9.

GHIGLIERI, M. P. (1987). 'Sociobiology of the Great Apes and the Hominid Ancestor'. *Journal of Human Evolution*, **16**: 319–57.

GLANDER, K. (1980). 'Reproduction and Population Growth in Free-ranging Mantled Howling Monkeys'. *American Journal of Physical Anthropology*, **53**: 26–36.

GOLDFOOT, D. A., H. WESTERBORG-VAN LOON, W. GROENEVELD, and A. K. SLOB (1980). 'Behavioral and Physiological Evidence of Sexual Climax in the Female Stump-tailed Macaque (*Macaca arctoides*)'. *Science*, **208**: 1477–9.

GOODALL, J. (1971). *In the Shadow of Man*. London: Collins.

GOODALL, J. (1986). *The Chimpanzee of Gombe*. Cambridge: Harvard University Press.

GOULD, S. J. (1976). 'Biological Potential vs. Biological Determinism'. In *The Sociobiology Debate*, A. Caplan (ed.). New York: Harper & Row.

——(1995). 'Male Nipples and Clitoral Ripples'. In *Adam's Navel*. London: Penguin.

GOWATY, P. A. (1995). 'False Criticisms of Sociobiology and Behavioral Ecology: Genetic Determinism, Untestability, and Inappropriate Comparisons'. *Politics and the Life Sciences*, **14**: 174–80.

——(1997). 'Sexual Dialectics, Sexual Selection and Variation in Mating Behavior'. In *Feminism and Evolutionary Biology: Boundaries, Intersections and Frontiers*, P. A. Gowaty (ed.). New York: Chapman & Hall.

——(in press). 'Forced Copulation in Birds: Occurrences and the CODE Hypothesis'.

HAIGHT, GORDON (ed.) (1954–78). *George Eliot Letters* (9 vols). New Haven, CT: Yale University Press.

HAMPSON, E. and D. KIMURA (1988). 'Reciprocal Effects of Hormonal Fluctuations on Human Motor and Perceptual-spatial Skills'. *Behavioral Neuroscience*, **102**: 456–9.

HARCOURT, A. (1996). 'Sexual Selection in Sperm Competition in Primates: What are Male Genitalia Good For?' *Evolutionary Anthropology*, **4**: 121–9.

——P. H. HARVEY, S. G. LARSON, and R. V. SHORT (1981). 'Testis Weight, Body Weight and Breeding Systems in Primates'. *Nature*, **293**: 55–7.

HARTUNG, J. (1976). 'On Natural Selection and the Inheritance of Wealth'. *Current Anthropology* **17**: 607–22.

HAUSFATER, G. and S. B. HRDY (eds.) (1984). *Infanticide: Comparative and Evolutionary Perspectives*. New York: Aldine.

HILL, K. and A. M. HURTAGO (1996). *Ache Life History: The Ecology and Demography of a Foraging People*. New York: Aldine de Gruyter.

——(1996). *Demography/Life Histories of Ache Foragers*. New York: Aldine de Gruyter.

——and H. KAPLAN (1988). 'Tradeoffs in Male and Female Reproductive Strategies Among the Ache, Part 2'. In *Human Reproductive Behaviour*, L. Betzig, M. Borgerhoff Mulder, and P. Turke (eds.). Cambridge, UK: Cambridge University Press.

HITE, S. (1976). *The Hite Report*. New York: MacMillan.

HRDY, S. B. (1986). 'Empathy, Polyandry and the Myth of the Coy Female'. In *Feminist Approaches to Science*, R. Bleier (ed.). New York: Pergamon.

——(1974). 'Male–male Competition and Infanticide Among the Langurs (*Presbytis entellus*) of Abu, Rajasthan'. *Folia Primatologica* **22**: 19–58.

——(1977). *The Langurs of Abu: Female and Male Strategies of Reproduction* Cambridge, MA: Harvard University Press.

——(1979). 'Infanticide Among Animals, a Review, Classification and Examination of the Implications for the Reproductive Strategies of Females'. *Ethology and Sociobiology*, **1**: 3–40.

——(1981). *The Woman that Never Evolved*. Cambridge, MA: Harvard University Press.

——(1988). 'The Primate Origins of Human Sexuality'. In *The Evolution of Sex*. R. Bellig and G. Stevens (eds.). New York: Harper & Row.

——(1990). 'Sex Bias in Nature and in History: A Late 1880's Reexamination of the 'Biological Origins' Argument'. *American Journal of Physical Anthropology*, **33**: 25–37.

——(1992). 'Fitness Tradeoffs in the History and Evolution of Delegated Mothering with Special Reference to Wet-nursing, Abandonment and Infanticide'. *Ethology and Sociobiology*, **13**: 409–43.

——and D. JUDGE (1993). 'Darwin and the Puzzle of Primogeniture: An Essay on Biases in Parental Investment After Death'. *Human Nature*, **4**: 1–46.

——and P. WHITTEN (1987). 'Patterning of Sexual Behavior. In *Primate Societies*, B. B. Smuts, D. L. Cheney, R. Seyfarth, R. Wrangham, and T. T. Struhsaker (eds.)'. Chicago IL: University of Chicago Press.

——C. JANSON, and C. VAN SCHAIK (1995). 'Infanticide: Let's Not Throw Out the Baby with the Bathwater'. *Evolutionary Anthropology*, **3**: 149–54.

HUBBARD, R., M. S. HENIFIN, and B. FRIED (eds.) (1979). *Women Look at Biology Looking at Women: A Collection of Feminist Critiques*. Cambridge, MA: Schenkman.

IZARD, M. K. (1983). 'Pheromones and Reproduction in Domestic Animals'. In *Pheromones and Reproduction in Mammals*, J. Vandenberg (ed.), New York: Academic Press.

JANSON, H. W. (1952). 'The Sexuality of Apes'. *Apes and Ape Lore in the Middle Age and the Renaissance*. London: Warburg Institute.

JONES, D. (1995). 'Sexual Selection, Physical Attractiveness and Facial Neoteny: Cross-cultural Evidence and Implications'. *Current Anthropology*, **36**(5): 723–48.

——and K. HILL (1993). 'Criteria of Facial Attractiveness in Five Populations'. *Human Nature*, **4**: 271–96.

——and S. B. HRDY (1992). 'Allocation of Accumulated Resources Among Close Kin: Inheritance in Sacramento, California, 1890–1984'. *Ethology and Sociobiology*, **13**: 495–522.

KEANE, B., W. P. J. DITTUS, and D. J. MELNICK (1997). 'Paternity Assessment in Wild Groups of Toque Macaques *Macaca sinica* at Polnnaruwa, Sri Lanka Using Molecular Markers'. *Molecular Ecology*, **6**: 267–82.

KARL, FREDERICK (1995). *George Eliot: Portrait of a Century*. New York: Norton.

KUMMER, H., W. GOTZ, and W. ANGST (1974). 'Triadic Differentiation: An Inhibitory Process Protecting Pair Bonds in Baboons'. *Behaviour*, **49**: 62–87.

LANCASTER, J. (1986). 'Human Adolescence and Reproduction'. In

Schoolage Pregnancy and Parenthood. J. Lancaster and B. Hamberg (eds.), 17–37. New York: Aldine de Gruyter.

LELAND, L., T. T. STRUHSAKE, and T. BUTYNSKY (1984). 'Infanticide by Adult Males in Three Primate Species of the Kibale Forest, Uganda: A Test of Hypothesis'. In *Infanticide: Comparative and Evolutionary Perspectives*. G. Hausfater and S. B. Hrdy (eds.). New York: Aldine de Gruyter.

LERNER, G. (1986). *The Creation of Patriarchy*. Oxford University Press.

——(1993). *The Creation of Feminist Consciousness*. NY: Oxford University Press.

LIESEN, L. T. (1995). 'Feminism and the Politics of Reproductive Strategies. Roundtable Commentaries and Reply'. *Politics and the Life Sciences*, **14**: 145–97.

LIPSCHITZ, D. L. (1992). 'Profiles of Oestradiol, Progesterone and Luteinizing Hormone During the Oestrous Cycle of Female *Galago senegalensis moholi*'. *Abstracts for the XIVth Congress of the International Primatological Society*, Strasbourg, 16–21 August.

LOVEJOY, O. (1981). 'The Origins of Man'. *Science*, **211**: 241–50.

MANSON, J. H. (1995). 'Female Mate Choice in Primates'. *Evolutionary Anthropology*, **3**: 192–5.

MARVAL, N. (1971). *The Case for Feminist Celibacy* (pamphlet). New York: The Feminists.

MASTERS, R. D. (1982). 'Is Sociobiology Reactionary? The Political Implications of Inclusive Fitness Theory'. *Quarterly Review of Biology*, **57**: 275–92.

MCARTHUR, L. Z. and D. S. BERRY (1983). 'Impressions of Baby-faced Adults'. *Social Cognition*, **2**: 315–42.

MCFARLAND, L. G. (1976). 'Comparative Anatomy of the Clitoris'. In *The Clitoris*. T. P. Lowry, and T. S. Lowry (eds.). St. Louis; MS: Warren Green.

MCHENRY, H. (1996). 'Sexual Dimorphism and Fossil Hominids and its Socioecological Implications'. In *The Archaeology of Human Ancestry*. James Steele and Stephen Shennan (eds.), 91–109. London: Routledge.

MORRIS, D. (1967). *The Naked Ape*. New York: Dell.

MORRIS, N. M. and J. R. UDRY (1970). 'Variations in Pedometer Activity during the Menstrual Cycle'. *Obstetrics and Gynecology*, **35**: 199–201.

MURDOCK, G. P. (1976). *Outline of World Cultures*. New Haven, CT. Human Relations Area Files.

NAKAMURA, M. (1990). 'Cloacal Protuberance and Copulatory Behavior of the Alpine Accentor (*Prunella collaris*)'. *The Auk*, **107**: 284–95.

PAGEL M. (1994). 'The Evolution of Conspicuous Oestrous Advertisement in Old World Monkeys'. *Animal Behaviour*, **47**: 1333–41.

PARISH, A. R. (1994). 'Sex and Food Control in the "Uncommon Chimpanzee": How Bonobo Females Overcome a Phylogenetic Legacy of Male Dominance'. *Ethology and Sociobiology*, **15**: 157–79.

——(1996). 'Female Relationships in Bonobos (*Pan paniscus*): Evidence for Bonding, Cooperation, and Female Dominance in a Male-philopatric species'. *Human Nature*, **7**: 61–96.

——and F. B. M. DE WAAL (1992). 'Bonobos Fish for Sweets: The Female Sex-for-Food Connection'. *Abstracts for the XIVth Congress of the International Primatological Society*, Strasbourg, 16–21 August.

PALOMBIT, R. (1992). 'Pair Bonds and Monogamy in Wild Siamangs (*Hylobates syndactylus*) and Whitehanded Gibbon (*Hylobates lar*) in Northern Sumatra'. Ph.D. thesis, University of California, Davis.

PARMIGIANI, S. and F. VOM SAAL (eds.) (1994). *Infanticide and Parental Care*. Chur, Switzerland: Harwood Academic Publishers.

PAXTON, NANCY (1991). *George Eliot and Herbert Spencer: Feminism, Evolutionism and the Reconstruction of Gender*. Princeton, NJ: Princeton University Press.

PEREIRA, M. E. and M. L. WEISS (1991). 'Female Mate Choice, Male Migration, and the Threat of Infanticide in Ringtailed Lemurs'. *Behavioral Ecology and Sociobiology*, **28**: 141–52.

PETRIE, MARION (1994). 'Improved Growth and Survival of Peacocks with More Elaborate Trains'. *Nature*, **371**: 598–9.

QUINN, NAOMI (1977). 'Anthropological Studies on Women's Status'. *Annual Review of Anthropology*, **6**: 181–225.

RIDLEY, M. (1993). *The Red Queen: Sex and the Evolution of Human Nature*. New York: MacMillan.

RIEDL, B. I. M. (1990). 'Morphologisch-metrische Merkmale des Mannlichen und Weiblichen Partnerleitbildes in Ihrer Bedeuturng fur die Wahl des Ehegatten'. *Homo*, **41**: 72–85.

RODSETH, L., R. W. WRANGHAN, A. HARRIGAN, and B. SMUTS (1991). 'The Human Community as a Primate Society'. *Current Anthropology*, **32**: 221–54.

ROSSI, A. (1995). 'A Plea for Less Attention to Monkeys and Apes, and More to Human Biology and Evolutionary Psychology'. *Politics and the Life Sciences*, August: 185–7.

SEARCY, J. W. A. and K. YASUKAWA (1989). 'Alternative Models of Territorial Polygyny in Birds'. *The American Naturalist*, **134**: 323–43.

SHERFEY, M. J. (1966/1972). *The Nature and Evolution of Female Sexuality*. New York: Vintage Books.

SHORT, R. D. (1979). 'Sexual Selection and its Component Parts, Somatic and Genital Selection, as Illustrated by Man and the Great Apes'. *Advances in the Study of Behavior*, **9**: 131–58.

SHOSTAK, M. (1981). *Nisa*. Cambridge, MA: Harvard University Press.

SIEFF, D. (1990). 'Explaining Biased Sex Ratios in Human Populations'. *Current Anthropology*, **21**: 25–48.

SILLEN-TULLBERG, B. and A. P. MOLLER (1993). 'The Relationship Between Concealed Ovulation and Mating Systems in Anthropoid Primates: A Phylogenetic Analysis'. *American Naturalist*, **141**: 1–25.

SINGH, D. (1993). 'Body Shape and Women's Attractiveness: The Critical Role of Waist-to-Hip Ratio'. *Human Nature*, **4**: 297–321.

SLOB, A. K., M. ERNSTE, and J. J. VAN DER WERFF TEN BOSCH. (1991). 'Menstrual cycle phase and sexual arousability in women!' *Archives of Sexual Behavior* **20**: 567–77.

SLOB, A. K., and J. J. VAN DER WERFF TEN BOSCH (1991). 'Orgasm in Nonhuman Species'. In *Proceedings of the First International Conference on Orgasm*, P. Kothari and R. Patel, ed. Bombay: VRP.

SLOB, A. K., W. H. GROENEVELD and J. J. VAN DER WERFF TEN BOSCH (1986). 'Physiological Changes during Copulation in Male and Female Stumptail Macaques (*Macaca arctoides*)'. *Physiology and Behavior* **38**: 891–5.

SMALL, M. (1988). 'Female Primate Sexual Behaviour and Conception: Are There Really Sperm to Spare?' *Current Anthropology*, **29**: 81–99.

——(1989). 'Female Choice in Nonhuman Primates'. *Yearbook of Physical Anthropology*, **32**: 103–27.

——(1993). *Female choices: Sexual Behavior of Female Primates.* Ithaca, NY: Cornell University Press.

SMITH, R. (1984). 'Human Sperm Competition'. In *Sperm Competition and the Evolution of Mating Systems*, R. L. Smith (ed.), 601–9. New York: Academic Press.

SMUTS, B. (1992). 'Male Aggression Against Women: An Evolutionary Perspective'. *Human Nature*, **3**: 1–44.

——(1995). 'The Evolutionary Origins of Patriarchy'. *Human Nature*, **6**: 1–32.

——and R. SMUTS (1993). 'Male Aggression and Sexual Coercion of Females in Nonhuman Primates and Other Mammals: Evidence and Theoretical Implications'. In *Advances in the Study of Behavior*, P. J. B. Slater, J. S. Rosenblatt, M. Miliniski, and C. T. Snowden (eds.). New York: Academic Press.

SOMMER, V. (1989). 'Sexual Harassment in Langur Monkeys (*Presbytis entellus*): Competition for Ova, Sperm and Nurture?' *Ethology*, **80**: 205–17.

——(1994). 'Infanticide Among the Langurs of Jodhpur: Testing the Sexual Selection Hypothesis with a Long-term Record'. In *Infanticide and Parental Care*, S. Parmigani and F. vom Saal (eds.). Chur, Switzerland: Harwood Academic Publishers.

Spencer, H. (1885). *The Principles of Sociology* (one of 5 vols between 1877 and 1896). New York: Appleton.

——(1904). *An Autobiography* (2 vols). London: Williams & Norgate.

STANISLAW, H. and F. J. RICE (1988). 'Correlation Between Sexual Desire and Menstrual Cycle Characteristics'. *Archives of Sexual Research*, **17**: 499–508.

SUSSMAN, R., J. CHEVERUD, and T. BARTLETT (1995). 'Infant Killing as an Evolutionary Strategy: Reality or Myth'. *Evolutionary Anthropology*, **3**: 149–54.

SYMONS, D. (1979). *The Evolution of Human Sexuality*. Oxford University Press.

——(1982). 'Another Woman that Never Existed'. *Quarterly Review of Biology*, **57**: 297–300.

TAKAHATA, Y. (1980). 'The Reproductive Biology of a Free-ranging Troop of Japanese Monkeys'. *Primates*, **21**: 303–29.

TAUB, D. (1980). 'Female Choice and Mating Strategies Among Wild Barbary Macaques (*Macaca sylvana*)'. In *The Macaques*, D. Lindberg (ed.). New York: Van Nostrand Rheinhold.

THORNHILL, R. and S. W. GANGESTAD (1993). 'Human Facial Beauty: Averageness, Symmetry and Parasite Resistance'. *Human Nature*, **4**: 237–69.

——and STEVE W. GANGESTAD (1996). 'The Evolution of Human Sexuality'. *TREE* **11**: 98–102.

——and N. W. THORNHILL (1983). 'Human Rape: An Evolutionary Analysis'. *Ethology and Sociobiology*, **4**: 137–73.

TRIVERS, R. (1972). 'Parental Investment and Sexual Selection'. In *Sexual Selection and the Descent of Man*, B. Campbell (ed.). Chicago, IL: Aldine de Gruyter.

TUTIN, D. (1975). 'Sexual Behavior and Mating Patterns in a Community of Wild Chimpanzees (*Pan troglodytes schweinfurthii*)'. Ph.D. dissertation, University of Edinburgh.

VAN NOORDWIJK, M. (1985). 'Sexual Behaviour of Sumatran Long-tailed Macaques (*Macaca fascicularis*)'. *Z. Tierpsychol*, **70**: 177–96.

VOLAND, E. (1984). 'Human Sex Ratio Manipulation: Historical Data from a German Parish'. *Journal of Human Evolution*, **13**: 99–107.

WALLEN, K. (1990). 'Desire and Ability: Hormones and the Regulation of Female Sexual Behavior'. *Neuroscience and Biobehavioral Reviews*, **14**: 233–41.

WALLIS, J. and Y. ALMASI (1995). 'A Survey of Reproductive Parameters in Free-ranging Chimpanzees (*Pan Troglodytes*)'. *Paper presented at the 18th Annual Meeting of the American Society of Primatologists*, 21–24 June.

WEST-EBERHARD, M. J. (1991). 'Sexual Selection and Social Behavior'. *Man and Beast Revisited*, M. H. Robinson and L. Tiger, (eds.). Washington, DC: Smithsonian Press.

——(1992). 'Behavior and Evolution'. In *Molds, Molecules and Metazoa: Growing Points in Evolutionary Biology*, pp. 56–79. P. R. Grant and H. S. Horn (eds.). Princeton, NJ: Princeton University Press.

WILSON, M. E., T. P. GORDON, and D. C. COLLINS (1982). 'Variation in Ovarian Steroids Associated with the Annual Mating Period in Female Rhesus (*Macaca mulatta*)'. *Biol. Reprod.* **27**: 530–9.

WOOD, J. (1994). *Dynamics of Human Reproduction: Biology, Biometry and Demography*. New York: Aldine de Gruyter.

WORTHMAN, C. M. (1978). 'Psychoendocrine Study of Human Behavior: Some Interactions of Steroid Hormones with Affect and Behavior in the !Kung San'. Ph.D. thesis, Harvard University.

WRANGHAM, R. (1993). 'The Evolution of Sexuality in Chimpanzees and Bonobos'. *Human Nature*, **4**: 447–80.

WRIGHT, R. (1994). *The Moral Animal: The New Science of Evolutionary Psychology*. New York: Pantheon.

——(1995). 'Demography and Life History of Free-ranging *Propithecus diadema edwardsi* in Ranomafana National Park, Madagascar'. *International Journal of Primatology*, **16**: 835–54.

ZUCKERMAN, S. (1932). *The Social Life of Monkeys and Apes*. London: Butler & Turner.

INDEX

Page numbers in **bold** refer to figures and those in *italic* refer to tables.

201